Ona

The Ancient Path
Understanding and
Implementing the Ways of our
Ancestors

Apetebii Iyalosa OlaOmi Osunyemi
Maat-Ra Efunlele Ajamu Alajo
Akalatunde

No part of this book may be reproduced without the written consent of the author.

Adupe (give thanks)

To YeYe Mi Osun, YeYe wa a ba won pe nimo,

To Baba Mi Obatala, Elejigbo

To Egun Idile Mi Nbelese Olodumare

To Moma, LaLeta Fields Morgan, My First Spiritual Preceptor

To Daddy, Willie James "Thunder" Morgan

To my siblings, Kerron, Sylvia, Willie,Jr. Stephanie, Shawn, Kita, Rochel, and Corey; who have been my companions in many lifetimes and agreed to walk this journey of life with me once more

To the Sistah sent to me by the Most High, Ayoka Adenlokun Tracey Gates, who never lets me forget that I am a Goddess

To my dawtas, these four Goddesses in Training:

Nailah, who saved my life and made me a Mommy

3

Kamilah, who taught me unconditional love
Asabi, who answered my prayers
'Fasoranti, who brought sweetness into my life
To my son,
 Asetunwa Bliss, who came into our lives to bring Divine Balance
To my newest dawta,
Nhubiyah Prophecy, born wearing a veil, who will speak to us of things yet to come
To the members of Onitoju Ona Agbani, Nashville, TN
MOST IMPORTANTLY...**To Ori Mi Iwo Ni**

A Note About the use of Bara or Wordsound Power in this Book

Throughout this work I have sought to include as much Afrikan language as possible. Therefore it is replete with Yoruba phrases. The book also contains KiSwahili. Most importantly, for Afrikans who were not born in Afrika I purposely include Afrikan-ized elements of English, sometimes called patois or ebonics. I do this for the same reason our Ancestors Afrikanized the language in the first place, so that we can retain the power of the spoken word, called "bara" in the Yoruba language. I also take the liberty of spelling some words differently so that they will house the vibration that I am trying to create with them. I include definitions within the text for words that are unfamiliar but here is a short list that you may wish to refer to.

Wholy- part of the Divine Whole, part of the ALL

Overstand- (thanks to my Rastafari family for this one) to truly comprehend a thing and thus internalize it

Brethren and Sistren- (also adopted from Rastafari) like minded males and like minded females respectively

Sistah- a like minded woman and close personal friend

5

Dawta- (also adopted from Rastafari) female offspring and/or a like minded woman, also the mate/wife of a brethren

Maafa- a KiSwahili term meaning "great disaster" generally attributed to have first been adopted by Afrikan scholar Oba T'Shaka as an accurate description of the rape, colonization, partitioning of Afrika by the nations of Europe and the enslavement of Afrikans that was a result of the above mentioned crimes.

Afrika and Afrikans- there is no letter 'c' in most Afrikan languages therefore to spell Afrika with a 'c' is an attempt to Anglicize the word or to make it more European.

Magick- as opposed to "magic" which is sleight of hand tricks used to amuse or entertain, magick denotes the ability to influence one's environment, this term is well-known to practitioners of the "Craft of the Wise" also known as witchcraft

Creatrix- the feminine essence of the Creator

Wombniverse- the womb of the Universe in which we all exist. I first encountered this phrase in the monumental work Sacred Woman, by the spiritual adept Queen Afua.

Shitstem-(another Rastafari term) an accurate description of the ways and mores of Western society and all the ills therein

The Yoruba words are defined as they are mentioned.

Chapter One

What is Ifa?

"Ifa asks what is truth ?
I ask what is truth ?
Truth is the wisdom of Olodumare
(Supreme Being)
guiding the Universe..."

Wholy Odu Osa'Tura

In its final analysis, all life bears witness to the fact attested to by this Odu. The Supreme Being is the Ultimate Controller and Designer of all life. In his search for the source of and reason for life, Western man has developed religion. According to the Afrikan religious scholar and sage Ra Un Nefer Amen, the word ["religion" is Latin in origin. "Religion" as a word can be broken down into two parts:'re' -'to do again' and 'ligare' – 'to tie back' . A religion is a method of tying back or re-binding ourselves with our Source.] A "religion" then is a system used to re- gain knowledge of the Ultimate Source and then re-connect oneself with that Source. Therefore a "religion" is of little use to those whose ethos or way of being does not include a belief in being disconnected from their own Divine Source. The Earth-based spiritual systems of our ancestors cannot rightfully be called religions as they originate from cultures which do not see themselves as disconnected from the Ultimate Reality.

Tens of thousands of years prior to the conception of "religions" our West Afrikan ancestors of the Anago people knew Olodumare (one of the many Yoruba names for the Supreme Being) as the source of all life and "that whose mat (or Self) spreads all over the Universe." Olodumare is the "Ultimate Reality", the sum total of all consciousness, the Divine Source from which all things emanate. Due to the fact that our human condition frequently causes us to forget that our true nature is Divine, our Ancestors developed methods to remind us of our Divinity and to assist us in accessing our Ase (Divine power). Ifa is one such method.

Ifa is a West Afrikan spiritual system practiced primarily by a people the ancients called Anago. The Anago are a Yoruba speaking people of Southwest Nigeria. Within West Afrika, each ethnic group (derogatorily called "tribes") has a spiritual system peculiar to its own conditions and ecosystem. Even though West Afrika is vast and ecosystems vary greatly from place to place, these spiritual systems are similar and inter-related, interdependent and interconnected just as the ethnic groups themselves are. Some of the other spiritual systems include Vodun of the Dahomey (Benin), Abasom of the Akom (Ghana), and the Nkisi of the Bakongo(Angola and Republic of the Congo).

Ifa is commonly known simply as "Yoruba" here in the West. Ifa and its spiritual siblings from neighboring cultures have many bi-cultural offspring as a result of the Maafa (KiSwahili term meaning "great disaster"; used to denote the rape of Afrika and the resulting slavery and colonization). Some of the more well-known and often mis-represented progeny are: Santeria, Lukumi, Voodoo, Obeah, Hoodoo, Conjure, Root-working, and to a much lesser degree the Black church. These offspring represent the mixture of Afrikan culture with Native American culture with elements of Eurocentric Christianity thrown in. Our enslaved ancestors used these spiritual systems to protect themselves and their families during captivity therefore hoodoo, voodoo, rootworking and any other practice that contained Afrikan spiritual elements were deemed wicked and evil by the slave masters. Years of oppression, domination, brainwashing , manipulation and scare tactics have caused Afrikans all over the world to view the practices in the same way as their former slave masters. It is difficult to find a modern Afrikan who is not afraid of the same systems his ancestors clung to. Anywhere Afrikans were enslaved in the Western world you will find traces of Ifa and/or its spiritual siblings from neighboring West

Afrikan cultures.

Ifa as a spiritual system has five major requirements its followers must meet. The first requirement is to be introspective; to seek the answers to your questions internally as opposed to outside yourself. The second requirement is to show respect and reverence for women, children and family; family is the basic unit for any community and therefore the most important institution in the universe, and must be uplifted and preserved. Thirdly, we must pay homage to elders; we must learn from the mistakes as well as the achievements of those who have walked the path of life before us. Fourth, it is of utmost importance to exercise patience; patience is seen as not only the ability to wait for the fullness of life to manifest itself in any given situation but also cultivating a cool, calm attitude towards all things in life. We must align ourselves with the forces of nature and understand that we are a part of the natural world. Last⑤we must frequently commune with the Spirit Realm, be it through prayer, deep thought, meditation, trance or any combination of these; communing with the Divine is essential for the Afrikan spirit; it keeps us conscious of our reality and allows us to stay aware of our connection with the Most High and therefore the Universe itself.

The path is both intricately complex and utterly simple at once. This is illustrated in what could be called the laws or "commandments" of Ifa. Ifa admonishes its adherents in the Wholy Odu (oral scripture) Ogbe Osa to

"Speak truth; do justice
Be kind and avoid evil.

For one who is righteous is supported by the Irunmole [forces of Light]"

Ifa devotees pursue Iwa Pele-Gentle character. Pursuing Iwa means that all devotees seek to handle all of life situations in a way that exhibits what our Ancestors called "pele" or gentleness. We are to handle life, ourselves and others with great care. We are to seek to remain gentle, peaceful and calm in the face of all that life has to offer us. According to our Ancestors, one who is able to remain calm or gentle makes the best decisions and therefore leads the best life. Ifa teaches that it is gentle character that "allows the rope of life to remain unbroken in one's hand". The ancient oral scriptures teach that the elder who has character "will enjoy good health and a long life". Gentle character is said to be the wife of wisdom and knowledge, meaning that the two go hand in hand. And "suuru ni baba 'wa" or "patience is the father of gentle character", meaning that the cultivation of patience gives birth to gentle character. Iwa Pele is the key to a pleasant life, to good health, to wisdom and to a long life.

Ifa has been in practice for some 20,000 years. At the time of this writing the Western year 2002, according to its annual calendar the Anago (Yoruba) nation itself is 10,045 years old. Those prehistoric civilizations that later merged and became the Anago were the first to practice this ancient way of life. As such, Ifa is the result of thousands of years of painstaking research and observation of nature and human's relationship to it, as well as, human's relationship with the Divine and other humans. The information gathered during this research is compiled in the sacred oral scripture of Ifa, known as Odu and in the D.N.A. of each melanated person as part of the "genetic library"; the storehouse of information passed from parent to child.

According to the primordial observations of our Ancestors, all things are a part of the Divine Whole. "All things" includes objects that most would consider inanimate. There is no spiritual line of demarcation between the so-called sacred and the so-called secular. Everything that is granted the power to exist is wholy, a part of the Divine Whole.

As parts of the Divine we never cease to be, we merely change forms. Our essence is spiritual. For example when one sets fire to a piece of wood and burns it until it is charcoal the piece of wood does not cease to be it merely changes form.

The essence of the wood remains the same. Being Divine, our essence exists simultaneously in both the spiritual and physical realms. The seat of our Divinity in the physical world is called Ori (Yoruba word meaning 'head'). As the name implies, the physical head is where the life force of a human being is concentrated. Thus the physical head is usually adorned and always protected. The Iponri is the seat of our Divinity in the spiritual world. The Iponri is the totality of all of our collective incarnations, it is our direct personal link to the spiritual realm, our tie to the Most High.

On the physical plane it is the Ori of each person that determines the path that that person is to take in life. That path has three separate elements. The first element is the akunleyan. The akunleyan is the part of our destiny that we choose before being born. The second element is the akunlegba. The akunlegba represents that part of our destiny that is determined by the choices we make once we are born. The final part is the ayanmo. The ayanmo is that part of our destiny that is predetermined, those things which are unalterable.

Ifa teaches that life is dynamic and destiny is no different, it is affected by life and may be altered by good or bad character. It is the choices you make that ultimately determine your destiny. Our Ancestors taught that before being born, each person kneels before Olodumare and chooses his akunleyan, the destiny he wishes to fulfill while in the physical world. Once we are born into the world we choose our akunlegba; the destiny that is determined by personal choices; day by day, minute by minute, second by second. The only inalterable parts of one's ayanmo are the date of birth and the "true" date of death. The distinction between the "true" date of death and the day a person actually dies is made to emphasize the fact that bad character can shorten one's life. Because so much of your destiny is determined by your character our ancestors said "Iwa nikan lo soro o" or "Character is all the is requisite"; meaning that character is what determines how your life will unfold. Your choices are led by your head, your thoughts, your mind, your Ori and so we are also taught in Ifa that "Ori lo ko won l'apere" or "Ori alone reaches completion", meaning that the nature of Ori is to seek fulfillment of your Divine destiny. All parts of our destiny are divine, from the choices we made kneeling before Olodumare in Orun (spiritual realm) to the choices we make on a daily basis, to the unalterable date of our physical death. Life in and of itself is Divine.

An eniyan is one chosen to experience a physical human life. Our Ancestors described those with gentle character as "real" human beings and those without it as those who "look like eniyan but do not act like enyian". From the perspective of our Ancestors it was unnatural to act without Iwa Pele. Once an eniyan is given birth to on the physical plane, it is her duty to revere those spiritual and physical forces that provided the body in which to live and a family line in which to be born. This is accomplished through reverence of one's family and one's family Egun. Egun is a Yoruba word meaning "bones". However the term is generally used to denote the spiritual force of one's bloodline Ancestors. Worship of our Egun keeps us in touch with the Divinity inherent on our own physical bodies as well as the miracle of our birth. Worship of our Egun teaches us to love ourselves, our features, and our genetic predispositions and to overstand that these things are Wholy.

Eniyan must also pay homage to the forces of nature that are the material that the physical body and (in finer particles) spiritual body are made of. The forces of nature are supplicated with orisa worship. The orisa are the "selected heads" of each natural element. Worship of the Orisa reminds us that nature is the Most High in action. This type of worship keeps us close to our Divine Source and allows us to learn the cycles of life and live according to them. When we learn the cycles we are then able to utilize them in order to increase our Ase(Divine Power/Lifeforce).

In addition to the spiritual practices listed above, each eniyan must revere his Ori and strive to know and align himself with his destiny in this lifetime. Reverence paid to Ori aligns us with our Iponri and reminds us that our essence is Divine and allows us not to fall prey to the pitfall of believing that we only have one life to live. We as Afrikans are eternal, worship of Ori assures us of this and allows the luxury of living life slowly and therefore assists us in living calmly with what our Ancestors called "suuru" or patience. Just as all other forms of life, humans pay homage to Olodumare (The Almighty) through our very existence.

Devotees of Ifa see life itself as constant ritual, with each breath and each action being a prayer of thanksgiving for our lives. Broken down to its lowest common denominator, Ifa is a state of mind, a perspective, a way of viewing life.

Ifa is the KNOWLEDGE (as opposed to the mere BELIEF) that our very essence is Divine. Being one with Olodumare, our core can be neither created nor destroyed. Our Ancestors spoke of this returning as "atunwa"; "the character comes again". Individuals are reborn into the same bloodline and while part of the spirit is reborn as the newborn (the ori) a portion of it also remains in Orun as part of the spirit world(the iponri).

In life, there is no need to fear. Eniyan are the children of Olodumare, ever under Wholy protection and guidance. All of life's occurrences bring us closer to the Most High. Things that we perceive as negative happen to teach us lessons necessary for our spiritual evolution. Positive things are the well-deserved results of the lessons we have already learned.

Chapter Two
Ancient Concept of the Most High

"We pay homage to Olodumare, the Ruler whose mat spreads all over the Universe..."
Ancient Iwure(prayer) to the Most High

Olodumare is generally accepted to be the Yoruba name for God. Olodumare then would be the Yoruba word to denote that being that is referred to as Yahweh, Jehovah, or Allah. This conclusion is blatantly incorrect as there is no ancient Afrikan God who coincides with the previously mentioned Western deities. Yahweh, Jehovah and Allah are remote patriarchal deities. They are, according to the holy books that they inspired "jealous", "wrathful", and even "vengeful". They use fear of retribution as the primary tool for ruling their children on Earth. According to the scriptures they inspired they reward blind acceptance (as seen the story of Abraham and Isaac) and punish intelligence and curiosity (as seen in the example Adamand Eve). They have one chosen people on Earth and therefore they give this group leave to treat other human beings as inferiors. They have also been known to divinely order the chosen group to commit wholesale genocide, and rape upon the other peoples of the Earth. Finally, they have given this chosen group "dominion" over the other species on Earth and these are to yield to the whims of the chosen people as well.

The God of the people "of the book" exists as a separate entity from his people. He sits apart from them and judges them from an authoritative position. The Earth, like his people is his creation and exists apart from him as well. He is only loosely connected to physical things and in fact generally condemns sexuality, desires, and wants as they are beneath him.

In light of this information, the God concept that exists in the minds of most Western people would have appeared ludicrous to the ancient Afrikans who were the first to conceptualize Divinity. Further, if one could have convinced them that such a deity existed, they surely would have judged him to be a spirit in need of evolution NOT reverence.

As such, Olodumare could not, cannot, and will never be the same as the God of Western mentality.

What, and who then is Olodumare? Our ancestors described this force as "that whose mat spreads all over the Universe". In ancient times, one's mat was where one slept, ate, prayed, made love and gave birth. The eni or mat was your own personal space. Olodumare then is that whose personal space is the Universe. Olodumare graciously shares this space with us all! Olodumare is the collective consciousness of all things. Olodumare is the material that all things are made of. Olodumare is also the supporter, the foundation, the "mat" of all things. We are all parts of Olodumare and Olodumare is the origin of all parts of us. Olodumare did not create the world but gave birth to it, so it is a part of Olodumare.

Olodumare, as all indigenous Afrikan deities, has male and female aspects. Olodumare houses both genders, as they both come from Olodumare and nothing is born without both. This does not imply androgyny nor is the Supreme Being a hermaphrodite. Olodumare is all male and all female at the same time. It is just as accurate to refer to Olodumare as "she" as it is to refer to her as "he".

Being made up of male and female components and having conceived and given birth, Olodumare does not condemn sexuality, physicality, wants or desires. The physical realm is just as Divine as the spiritual realm and the two act in conjunction with one another. According to Ifa, the spiritual realm and the physical realm are two halves of the same gourd or calabash. Therefore the physical and spiritual aspects of ourselves, our bodies, our personalities are two Divine parts of our Divine Selves and act in conjunction with each other.

The feminine aspect of Olodumare is apparent in the name itself . "Ol" means owner, "odu" means womb and "mare" means rainbow. "The owner of the womb of the rainbow" would be the translation of the name as a whole. This translation contains the word "odu" which is the Yoruba word for womb, repository, or carrier. This word is also use to denote the history of the Yoruba people as it is held in the oral traditions kept by the priest and priestesses. In Anago cosmology, the totality of existence is within a womb. Everything takes place within the Wombniverse. And anything that is about to happen, or anything that is in the process of happening was given birth to. Not only are people, animals, and plants brought forth by some sort of birthing process, but according to our Ancestors so are the situations, processes and challenges that make up our daily lives. All things come from one womb or another.

Olodumare is only one name and only one aspect of those elements that are parts of the Supreme Being. Because it is considered to be more similar in form to physical beings than some of the other aspects it is one of the more well known names and aspects. Another well known name and aspect of the Most High is Olorun (the owner of the spirit realm).

Olodumare guides the Universe by example. Because Olodumare gave birth to the world as opposed to creating it, the earth, human beings and everything in the world is a part of Olodumare and does not exist separately from her. By sharing all of himself, and in essence using himself to create, maintain and sustain us; he teaches us how to treat one another. Therefore, all societies devoted to a belief in Olodumare are communalistic. Olodumare has not chosen one specific group of humans or even on particular species of Earthly thing as her cosmic "favorite". Olodumare allows all to share in the blessings of life equally and also strikes everyone with some of life's curses as well. Olodumare does not punish those who seek "the knowledge of good and evil" for she is life and life rewards curiosity and intellect. Olodumare is does not control her children with fear of a torturous afterlife if they do not follow her laws. Those who do not follow Universal law make their own lives a daily "hell".

Olodumare is the benevolent, loving, giving and caring Universe and the Force that created that Universe. Olodumare is all things known and unknown, all things seen and unseen. She is all of existence as well as those things that do not exist. Olodumare is also all of the hardships, obstacles, and difficulties of life; for without those things our spirits would not be equipped to evolve to the next level.

Chapter Three
Who Are The Orisa?

"They were praising the Diviners
And the Diviners were praising
Orisa!"
Various Odu

Olodumare is all things, the entire Wombniverse. Olodumare is not only the power that causes us to be but Olodumare is us also, the totality of all things. What we see as humans, animals, plants, insects is but this same power diluted, diffused, less concentrated. As Olodumare diffuses Itself and makes the journey from spiritual to physical It takes many forms. Therefore our Ancestors taught that there are many levels of Olodumare, many levels of the Wombniverse, and many levels of human beings as well. As humans there are certain forms of Olodumare that are closer to our level and therefore more accessible to us. Our Ori is one form, our Ancestors another form and the Orisa are yet another form.

Many anthropologists and missionaries have referred to Ifa (and other nature revering spiritual systems) as polytheism, animism and/or fetishism. These terms reveal misconceptions about ancient belief systems that arise from European cultural arrogance. When Europeans study the belief systems of Afrikans and other people of color they do so within the context of White supremacy. The foundation of White supremacy is a belief that the melanated people of the Earth were uncivilized before contact with Europeans. White supremacy purports that these people had no culture, no spirituality, no philosophy of their own. The supposition that the majority of the Earth's population (because melanated people, people of color, are the global majority) lived in spiritual, mental, and technological "darkness" for billions of years until the coming of the Europeans(who are the global minority) is ridiculous. However, it is a belief that is in keeping with the teachings of that philosophical monster that is the bastion of White supremacy; Eurocentric Christianity. The reader will recall in the chapter entitled "The Ancient Concept of the Most High" that all Eurocentric Gods have a chosen people. Europeans fancy themselves the chosen people of the Gods they have fashioned. As such it is their duty and God-given right to subdue, to colonize and if they feel so inclined to destroy the other peoples of the Earth. This destruction is divinely ordained as anything that came before their God is an affront to him. Therefore ancient ways of life are seen as things primitive, unlearned melanated people did before we were saved, and civilized by the God's chosen people; the Europeans. The irony of the belief that Europeans were the bringers of culture to the earth is that close examination and study of European culture (including American culture) reveals that European culture is the offspring of Afrikan culture. That is to say that most things we consider to be European are but imitations of ancient Afrikan societies that were pillaged by the earliest European invaders. European culture is built on Greco-Roman philosophy and Greco-Roman philosophy is an adulteration of ancient KMTic (now called Egyptian) philosophy. A deeper explanation of this truth can by found by studying the book Stolen Legacy by George G.M. James. The bastion and pinnacle of Eurpoean culture, Eurocentric Christianity is an adulteration of

Afrikan spirituality.

For clarity, any form of Christianity that practices under the edicts of the Council of Nicea, is Eurocentric Christianity and has White Supremacy at its core. The purpose of the Council was to remove all Afrikan elements from the origins of Christianity in order to justify the enslaving of Afrikans and the stealing of the land and other natural resources of Afrika. All churches whose root is the Catholic church or the Anglican church, (and all Protestant churches were founded by either a split from the Anglican church or a split from a protestant church which had split from the Anglican church) practice Eurocentric European Christianity. In short, all churches in the Western hemisphere and the majority of those found elsewhere are perpetuating white supremacy and all of the evils therein.

Judaism and hence Christianity and Islam are re-workings of the ancient spiritual system of Ethiopia. Ethiopia is the oldest Afrikan High Culture and is the mother of KMT (Egypt). The creation as espoused in Genesis was stolen from the Shabaka stone of Ethiopia. Abraham who is given the title "Father of monotheism" did not begin to teach and preach monotheism until he returned from his sojourn to KMT where monotheistic Afrikans had revered the Divine Whole, the One, the All for millennia. The commandments accredited to Moses were stolen from the 142 negative confessions of Maat that were foundation of life in KMT. The story of the immaculate conception and birth of Jesus were stolen directly from the walls of the Temple of Dendera in KMT. The only historical personage who fits the description of Jesus is an Ethiopian member of an ancient group of Afrikan spiritual preceptors known as the Essene. His name was Yeshua ben Pendera (It must be noted here that the name Jesus could not have existed as the Hebrew language contains no 'j'.) He was initiated as an Essene in KMT, which was the home of the Essene Mystery System. Like many righteous Afrikan men to follow (we pay homage to their courageous spirits) he was murdered by hanging. According to historical record the lynching took place in Palestine. The charge was teaching the "foreign doctrines" of the Essene to the people there.(For further evidence of these facts see Afrikan Origins of Major World Religions, edited by Dr. Yosef ben Jochannan.) All of these facts were deemed unworthy to be a part of the Christian doctrine decided upon by the Council of Nicea. How ironic it is that missionaries pour into Afrika every day with the intent of saving the very people who taught the world what it meant to be "saved", to be Wholy, to be righteous!

During the colonial era Europeans stormed in to Afrika by the thousands. Many studies were undertaken and many treatises were written on the ways and mores of the peoples of Afrika. Most of these studies were used to justify the enslavement of Afrikan people, and the looting of Afrika's vast natural and financial resources. The purpose of the research that occurred during this time was to further the diabolical causes of Eurocentricism, White Supremacy, and male chauvinism. The conclusions drawn from this biased research still form the basis of most of the world's view of Afrikan spirituality till this day. A prime example of this was a conversation I had with a newspaper reporter while I was in Nigeria. He wanted to know why I would choose to practice Ifa, when it was wicked and backward and the priest and priestess in the tradition only wanted to take money from people. I asked him to look at the home I was staying in, it was the home of an Ifa priest. The dwelling was simple two story concrete building with no running water and sporadic electricity. It was a typical Nigerian home. Then I asked him to look across the road at the 4 level, multi-bedroom brick mansion (and I do not use this term loosely). The mansion was furnished with massive tanks to provide running water and a generator to provide electricity constantly and the hedges on the sidewalk in front of it read "Jesus is Lord". The mansion was owned by a local preacher. I then asked him which one of these men looks as if they are taking the people's money. The reporter, like the rest of us who have received a Western education was a victim of Eurocentric Christianity. We have been programmed to believe that there must be an inherent evil in those systems that existed prior to Eurocentric Christianity. Many of us, just like the reporter in Nigeria, automatically assume that Afrikan spiritual practices are backwards and wicked or are scams to take money from others. Just like the reporter, we rarely take the time to stop and look at the harm that has been and still is being done to us by Christianity, Judasism and Islam. When I chose to practice Ifa my small town Black Southern family was outraged and claimed that I was endangering my soul. I asked them how many thousands innocent people have been killed and are being killed every day for the sake of

Christianity, Judaism and Islam and how many have been killed for Ifa? If we chose to believe our eyes as opposed to what we are told we should believe, which system appears to be wicked and barbaric and backward?

Even though the modern world claims to have advanced past these narrow- minded ways of thinking, the research undertaken during colonization is still accepted as the dictum on the cultures that were studied during that time. Great is the necessity for Afrikan scholars from around the globe to conduct research of their own. For now this author will do her level best to debunk the myths that run rampant about Ifa.

Ifa is not polytheistic. It can be described (as can most ancient religions) as a "diffused monotheism". A phrase coined by Afrikan scholar and author John S.

Mbiti in his monumental work African Religions and
Philosophies : or , by my own phrase "uni -ism". Both phrases describe the way of thinking the purports that all things exist only as a part of Olodumare. Olodumare is multi-faceted and each part of herself falls under the jurisdiction of a Cosmic Being, a force of nature a "selected head; an orisa.

Ifa is not animism. Animism is not an Afrikan word so it cannot accurately be used to describe an Afrikan phenomenon. Animism is "the belief that all natural objects, as trees and stones, possess an inherent spiritual being or soul". Ifa teaches that the life force in all things is a part of Olodumare. All things are part of a living, breathing, interconnected and interactive whole. Life is not as simple as everything having a soul. Like a giant crocheted blanket each thread is intricately connected to the other thread, all parts of life touch every other part. In the words of Daniel Quinn in The Story of B, "all of life is of a piece".

Ifa is not fetishism. A "fetish" is "any inanimate object that is worshipped or regarded with superstitious awe". Oddly, according to this definition Christianity with its crucifixes and rosaries, Judaism with its Torah and Mogan Dawud (Star of David) and Islam with the Quran, the Ka'aba and the Well of Zamzam should be classified as fetishism. Ifa recognizes that all things house vibrations. It is through the vibration of our molecules that we live and take our various shapes. Our Ancestors used the vibrations of natural objects to maintain alignment with the Universe. Therefore if one is out of alignment with his destiny, a particular stone, a specific color or the bark of a certain type of tree may assist one in returning his vibration to its correct level. The ways of accessing this natural Ase (power) varied according to the situation. The natural object was always thanked for having assisted in the individual's return to Divine alignment. All of nature was seen as a part of the Divine family of Olodumare; so thanking a stone, a tree or an animal was tantamount to thanking a sibling for reminding you of the instructions of your mother and saving you from a reprimand.

A large portion of what European observers could not comprehend or overstand about Ifa is the multi-faceted nature of Olodumare. The manifold dimensions of Olodumare are grouped together within complex forces. The most well-known group of these forces are the Orisa. The science of orisa worship is a labyrinthine mixture containing among many other sciences, the sciences of color therapy, reflexology, herbology, and numerology. There are as many orisa as there are natural forces. However, when asked to cite a particular number of orisa our Ancestors generally stated that there were 401. There are 200 orisa that sit on the right hand of Olodumare and 200 that sit on the left. The extra one is sometimes believed to be Esu who is the orisa who dispenses Ase (Divine power) who sits in the middle. (Some other scholars have stated that it is Ogun, the deity of iron who is the extra one.) The orisa on the right hand are generally thought to be spirits of Light who are positive forces, while the ones on the left are believed to be spirits of Darkness who are negative forces. Each group has a right to exist and all are necessary for life, as we know it to continue. Our Ancestors believed that each situation, person and thing had both positive and negative aspects and that true harmony was achieved with the balance of the two.

Each orisa has a natural manifestation such as, rivers, mountains or trees. There is a particular town in Ancient Yorubaland in which the worship of each one originated. Every orisa also finds expression in a myriad of human, animal and plant life forms. Because each town has an orisa that is peculiar to it, originally West Afrikan family groups and hence villages and empires found themselves under the protection of a particular orisa. Therefore, the priestly class in each village devoted itself to studying the Awo (mysteries/magick) of the orisa whose protection their village fell under. This practice took a lifetime (or lifetimes) as each deity has a complete oral encyclopedia of herbal knowledge, folklore, incantations, prescriptions, prayers, songs, dances, poetry, cloth and clothing, jewelry and amulets, sacred symbols, masks, and carvings devoted to it.

With the Maafa in which millions of Afrikans were captured and placed in captivity our ties to our villages were severed and the priests and priestesses were thrust together. This catastrophe forced them to merge all of their wisdom into one common practice. Maafa marked the beginning of Ifa in its current Western state. This form is known as Orisa Worship, Santeria ("worship of the saints "), Sango Baptiste, Lukumi, Macumba and a myriad of other names. As stated previously, many of the practices also added Native America elements that were introduced to the practitioners on these shores. These new practices were also forced to include Eurocentric Christian elements which allowed the Ancestors to camouflage their practices and thereby survive in an environment created to destroy them.

In the West, with no villages to denote which orisa protected and defended us more emphasis was placed upon the "orisa that rules one's head". It was now incumbent upon each individual to form a personal relationship with that deity that was predominant in her personality. Our Ancestors continued the practice of determining upon the eighth day after birth for girls and the ninth day for boys which orisa each child belonged to. This was achieved using that most ancient of Ifa's tools, D'Ifa or divination. By knowing the child's orisa the parents could determine how the child could access those forces that would protect him and assist him in aligning his life with the mind of Olodumare. This information also gave the community valuable insight into the child's personality as well as what colors, scents, metals, stones, herbs, foods, et cetera were good for him and which ones were not. In knowing his orisa the community could know the child even before he began to know himself.

The orisa that "rules" your head is the Cosmic Force that asserts itself the strongest in your spiritual self. All of us are made up of all of the orisa but there are two in particular that come to the fore of our Ori in each lifetime. These two are our mother and father orisa and they guide, and protect us for the duration of this life. When we knelt before Olodumare and chose our destinies, these were the forces that pledged to assist us in every endeavor. Knowing these orisa allows us to see more clearly the paths in life that would be most advantageous for us. It is only through D'Ifa that one can truly know who her orisa is, although most have an inkling prior to having a divination. Your orisa is the force that matches your personality type most closely. Following is a partial listing of orisa and the ways in which they manifest.

A Partial Listing of Orisa and other Spiritual Forces

ORI

Ori is the cosmic spiritual force than animates each thing in this particular lifetime. Ori is the head of all other orisa and it is said that no orisa blesses one without the consent of her Ori. Ori is your consciouness, your spirit, your "first mind". Pronounced "oh-ree".

EGUN

Egun is the force of deceased relatives. Egun contains the moral standard of the human race. They have lived and so they know how to live properly. Egun is the concept of lineage, the science of geneology, and the concept of family. All are children of Egun as all have Ancestors.
Pronounced "eh-goon".

EGUNGUN

Egungun is the force of Egun that has been elevated to a higher level. An Ancestor who lived a good life while on Earth and continued to assist his family once he died and returned to the Spirit Realm is then elevated to Egungun. Pronounced "eh-goon-goon".

These three spiritual forces occupy a space in the cosmology that is different from the Orisa. They are still active in our lives and as such must be duly ritualistically revered and supplicated. The part they play in our lives is fine tuned as it is personalized for this particular incarnation. For example, we do not share our Ori with anyone else and our Egun and Egungun are peculiar to our blood relatives and our ancestral lineage. So while it is true that Egungun is an Orisa: a "selected head" of Egun it is not the same type of force as the other deities.

ESU

Esu is the dispenser of Ase or life-force to all things. Esu is also known as Elegba or Legba. Esu is the conduit through which the Ase of Olodumare must pass so that all things
can use it. Esu exists outside of good and evil and is therefore seen

being a "trickster". Esu is represented by chance, choice, and decisions. He is naturally manifested by crossroads, mice and rats. His vibration is in laterite stone and the colors red and black together. His number is three. Those born with a preponderance of Esu are practical jokers who have illusive, enigmatic personalities. They are very playful, and childlike and also highly sexual. Pronounced "eh- shoo".

OBATALA

Obatala is the most ancient Earthly cosmic force. Obatala is also known as Orisanla. He is the bright white light out of which all material things are created. His name means "King of the White Cloth". He is the force of the creative impulse as well as the force of purity. He is the desire for purity of mind, soul and body. He shaped the first human beings and he shapes each fetus in the womb. He is DNA. He is enlightenment, upright behavior, and peacefulness. He is naturally manifested in mountains, elephants, snails and the white hair of old age. His vibration is found in pewter and the color white. His number is eight. (It has been stated that Obatala is Caucasian. Ifa was developed by West Afrikan people in West Afrika and an un-colonized people always conceive of the Divine as having the same physical characteristics they do. To state that Obatala was perceived as Caucasian by the Ancients is merely a symptom of the same psychopathic racist mentality that leads Europeans to teach that Yeshua ben Pendera [Jesus] was white when all scriptures written about him as well as all descriptions of him by his contemporaries say he was not.) Children of Obatala are artistic and creative. They are usually purists and pursue perfection, righteousness and purity in all of their endeavors. Doing what is right is of EXTREME importance to them. They generally must have very pure diets (they must eat natural foods with no man-made components) or they will suffer from digestive disorders and/or other diet-related illnesses. They are good orators and public speakers. They require a great deal of solitude in order to fulfill their destinies. They think very logically and generally are good problem solvers and can be know-it-alls as well. They will suffer from headaches, acne, insanity and confusion when not in alignment with their destinies. They must be very protective of their heads at all times as Obatala rules the head and they should never wear black on their heads nor be our after midnight without something white on their heads. All differently-abled individuals are seen as special creations of Obatala and are sacred to him. Pronounced "oh-bah-tah-lah".

Olokun

Olokun is the most ancient cosmic force of water. His name means the "owner of the ocean". He is the force of maintaining life through nurturing by feeding. He is represented in deep, contemplative thought and all things unfathomable. He is naturally manifested in the ocean, especially the bottom of the ocean. He is the father of all waters on the Earth and as such was the original owner of the Earth whose ownership he acquiesced to Obatala. All of the creatures that live on the ocean floor are symbols of Olokun. His vibration is also found in the colors red and white together, indigo blue and white together and indigo blue alone. According to the Awo of Oyotunji Village ,Olokun is the father Orisa of Afrikan(Black) people. Children of Olokun are mysterious deep thinkers. Like children of Obatala they require solitude in order to maintain inner harmony. They are very good at counseling and getting to the core of any matter. They commune with spirits often and generally start doing so at a very young age. They constantly battle to find balance between the spiritual realm and the physical realm. They often have prophetic dreams and visions and are usually psychic as well. They should guard against living too much of their lives in the spiritual realm and therefore neglecting themselves physically Our brethren and sistren in Haiti say that it is to the watery abyss of Agwe(the

Vodun equivalent to Olokun) that we return at death before our spirits go home to Guine (Afrika/heaven). Pronounced "oh-low-koon".

YEMONJA

Yemonja is the most ancient force of mothering. Yemonja is also known as Yemaya. Her name means "mother of the children of the fish" and from an evolutionary perspective we are all children of the fish. She is the female portion of Olokun. She is the force of nurturing and breastfeeding or sustaining the life of another with your own life force. She is the origin of those areas of womanhood that are the domain of women only; menstruation, birth, mothering, and nursing. She is the force of tradition as a people's acceptable way of being and doing. She is naturally manifested in the Ogun river (Nigeria's largest river) and by the top layers of the ocean and the waves of the ocean in the West. Her vibration can be found in clear crystal, molasses, fishes, and coral. Her colors are any shade of blue and crystal. The moon is also a manifestation of Yemonja especially in its crescent aspect. Her number is seven. According to my spiritual father Oluwo 'Fatayi 'Fagbenro of Abeokuta, Nigeria her children should not eat fish as this is like eating one's own children. For those of us who are survivors of the Maafa in the West (Afrikan Americas, Afrikan Caribbeans, Afro-Cubans, Afro-Brazilians et cetera) it was Yemonja and Olokun who brought us safely to these shores and it was they who called us home when we jumped or were thrown overboard. Those whose heads are ruled by Yemonja are stern, strict disciplinarians who are also loving and nurturing. They are the keepers of tradition and like to do things in the most orthodox manner possible. They exude "Mama energy" whether or not they have children and seem to always have the best interests of their friends and loved ones at heart. They must guard against being in relationships in which they are nurturing and loving and not being nurtured and loved in return. Female children of Yemonja must guard against choosing mates who are seeking a mother figure. Children of Yemonja tend to carry their disappointments, hurts, and emotional scars as excess weight and therefore must guard against obesity. Keep in mind however, that most Afrikan women are not meant to be a size three and that a voluptuous healthy body is a thing of beauty. Her children are drawn to the moon and usually do not sleep well when She is full. They should gather moonwater and use it as Ori guides them. (Place a clear container of pure water outside so that the light of the full moon shines in it, bring it inside before sunrise.) Pronounced "yeh-mon-jah".

OSUN

Osun is the force of attraction between opposites and the balance felt between complementary opposites. Her name means "the source". She is the sexual act and the reproduction that occurs due to attraction. She is the force of harmony. Harmony is felt as love, seen as beauty, known as attraction. She is the most ancient creatrix of marriage and any partnership that exists for the continuance and good of human life. She is the origin of female sexuality. She is the force of self-evaluation, and intuition. She is manifested in the enjoyment of life that is seen in fashion, dance, and art. She is the concept of the acquisition of wealth by using hard work and discipline to create more than you need. She is the sharing of this wealth with others. She is naturally manifested by the Osun river in Osogbo ,Nigeria and by all other rivers and bodies of fresh water here in the West. She is manifested in honey, cinnamon and fresh water fish. Her vibration is found in the colors yellow, orange, and gold in any shade and in the metal brass. Her number is five. She is also the feminine art of witchcraft, as the head of the Iyaami Aje; the Yoruba witches. Originally the Old English word "wicce" pronounced "witch" meant "wise woman". This is the connotation used in the Iyaami Aje concept as well. A wise woman is one who uses all of the forces of nature to her advantage and the advantage of those she loves, Osun is the leader of such women. She is woman as a force to be reckoned with, sought after, and revered. Her number is five. Osun's children have magnetic personalities and are also usually physically attractive; they are irresistible people. They are sweet, kind, giving and loving but vicious, vindictive and even deadly when angered. They must guard against depression due to the world not being as lovely and sweet as they know it could be. They must be careful not to use their sexuality as a weapon. Children of Osun are usually the life of the party and/or the center of the community. They adore things of beauty and will become gloomy if forced to be in "ugly" (visually or energetically) places for long periods of time. They love to adorn themselves and their surroundings. They also love sweet foods and must be careful not to fall prey to sugar addiction and the diseases that come with it. They love to "party" and are "social butterflies". They are attracted to the occult and the darker aspects of spirituality. They can be arrogant, conceited, and self-centered. They must guard against being used in love relationships and also protect themselves from the jealousy and envy they inevitably inspire. Pronounced "aw-shoon".

OYA

Oya is the force of change that allows the Earth and her inhabitants to evolve. She is also known as Yansa. Her name means "to rip or to tear". She is the fierce, protective instincts of women. She is the force of male/female equality but NOT same-ness. She is the tenacity of the human spirit as exhibited in the desire to continue to be born, to die and be born again. As such she is the mother of Egungun and the mother of Ancestral Reverence. She is naturally manifested in the Niger river in Nigeria and by cemeteries, the wind, tornadoes, fire and natural disasters in the West. The buffalo and Native American Buffalo Women also symbolically represent Oya. She is the graceful, fluid movement of dance. Her vibrations are found in the colors purple, maroon, black and the metal copper. Her number is nine. Children of Oya are usually tall and graceful. They are generally magnificent dancers. They have striking physical characteristics and unforgettable personalities. They commune with ancestral beings effortlessly and are not easily frightened. They have very profound dreams quite often and should keep a dream journal. Those who do not dream at night have intense waking dreams that they should pay attention to. Daughters of Oya may exhibit the type of physical aggressiveness that is generally reserved for males in Western society. Oya's children like combat and are competent warriors. Women who grow beards are usually daughters of Oya. They should guard against being aloof, defensive and overly combative. Pronounced "oh-yah".

SANGO(Kawo kabiesile)

Sango is the force of strength and perseverance that causes man to strive for correctness and righteousness. He is also known as Chango and Oba Koso. After we say his name we always say "Kawo kabiesile or its shortened form kabiyesi", both of these phrases mean "greetings to his majesty" and denote Sango's kingly nature and the fact that the fourth Alaafin (king) of Oyo was an incarnation of Sango. He is the power of truth and the support that the Universe lends to those who are truthful. He is the force of using strategy to overcome the negativity of life. He is the origin of male sexuality. He is the force of fatherhood as a life giving, protective, loving Universal power. He is the force of messianic deliverance manifested as those who lead others to the Divine. He is the force of charisma. He is naturally manifested in thunder, lightening, rain and fire (which he received from Oya who is one of his wives). His vibration is in the colors red and white together as well as cedar wood (or parts of any tree struck by lightening) and the color purple that the sky becomes when lightening strikes. His sacred cities in Yoruba land are Koso and Oyo. He is manifested in the sound of drumming as well as drummers themselves. His numbers are six and four. Children of Sango are devastatingly beautiful. They are powerfully attractive. They are smooth talkers and natural charmers. They can use their words to get almost anything. They must guard against being promiscuous, as they will always have people throwing themselves at them. Sango's children are master dancers and/or drummers. They abhor liars and lying but may frequently bend the truth themselves. They must guard against being pathological liars. They must also be careful not to brood over the negative aspects of life. Children of Sango also favor bodily adornment and are usually well groomed and well dressed. They generally have a positive self-image. They are natural strategists and planners. They love to talk and network. Pronounced "shon-go".

OGUN

Ogun is the force of efficiency, invention, and solitude. He is the human tendency to struggle for a better more abundant life. He is the force of war and wholistic technological advancement. He is the force of territorialism. He is represented in the human ability to use nature to make mental images manifest or invention. He is naturally manifested in the forest, blacksmiths and black dogs. His vibration can be found in the metal iron and in the colors green and black together. His number is seven. He is the owner of Ire (the blessings of life). He gains this Ire through work as he works ceaselessly. Children of Ogun are solitary people who enjoy spending time alone. When faced with trouble or negativity they "retreat to the forest" by going within. They must guard against using physical aggression and/or intimidation to control others. Ogun's children are the "strong silent type"; they are also dependable and reliable. Males whose heads are ruled by Ogun may suffer from impotence or infertility and therefore must take preventive measures against these dis-eases. Children of Ogun are creative and enjoy working with their hands. Ogun's children must guard against acting hastily. Pronounced "oh-goon".

OSOOSI
Osoosi is the force of the ability to seek and to follow anything to its

logical conclusion. Osoosi is also known as Ochoosi. He is the manner in which this force allows us to hunt and track as well as to locate the Divine in ourselves. He is the force of being skillful in one's craft. He is the force of manifesting a harmony with nature and the realization that all animals are our brothers. He is naturally manifested in the forest, and the hunter especially the Native American brave and Native American culture in general. His vibration is found in the bow and arrow and the vibrations of the colors orange and blue together. Children of Osoosi are highly attracted to nature and the outdoors. They feel a oneness with all of creation. They are extremely focused when working towards a goal and as such must guard against being narrow-minded or having a one-track mind. They are able to break any situation down to its lowest common denominator.

They are naturally curious and inquisitive. Pronounced "oh-show-shee".

OSANYIN

Osanyin is the force of the harmony between plant life and human life. He is the ability to heal and cure illness. He is the knowledge of the properties of plants. He is the life-force and curative powers stored within plants. He is represented by herbalists, "witch doctors", and shamans. He is naturally manifested in plants; especially healing herbs and in the science of medicine. His vibration is found in the forest and in the color green. Children of Osanyin were the world's original doctors. They have "green thumbs" and an inherent ability to communicate with and understand plants. They are most at home when growing things, or taking care of things they have grown. They are aware of the fact that any plant that can cure can also harm and so they are usually well balanced. Pronounced "oh-sigh-een"

OBALUAIYE

Obaluaiye also known as Babaluaiye is the force of cleanliness and purification and the results of filth. His names mean "king of the world" or "father of the world" respectively. He is the force of contagious dis-ease and its ability to destroy or scar the physical body. He is the desire to use cleanliness as preventive medicine. He is the wholistic understanding of illness as the result of microscopic organisms combined with physical, spiritual, or mental dis-ease. He is the force of homeopathy. He is naturally manifested in flies, and mosquitoes and the forest. His vibration is found in the colors black, white, and maroon together. Children of Obaluaiye, like children of Osanyin love working with the Earth. Obaluaiye's children introduced inoculation to the world. Yoruba priests of Obaluaiye were the inventors of the small pox vaccination. They are natural gardeners, farmers and ecologists. Like children of Obatala they also require purity in diet to ward off sickness. They have a tendency to be aloof but are loyal and faithful to their close friends. They are resilient and able to withstand great hardships with grace. They are EXTREMELY introspective and require periods of "hibernation" to maintain spiritual alignment and sanity. Pronounced "oh-bah-loo-eye-ay".

ORUNMILA

Orunmila is the force of wisdom. He is the force of those things KNOWN rather than BELIEVED. He is the ability to commune with Olodumare and the power to know all things as a vessel of Olodumare. He is the force of knowledge. He is the power of humans to create symbols such as numbers and letters. He is the force of salvation from negativity through knowledge of one's higher Self. He is the force of divination. He is the force of recording events. He is history as the remembrance of past events and their significance to the present. He is the force of culture as the way a certain people live life. He is the force of memory. He is naturally manifested in the West Afrikan palm tree and its nuts. His vibration is found in the colors yellow and green together or green and brown together. His number is sixteen. Children of Orunmila are wise, thoughtful and quiet. They usually ponder over matters before speaking on them. They are powerful but gentle, strong but tender. They are generally delicate and may be sickly as children, therefore encouraging the development of mental over physical capacity. They have wonderful sometimes, photographic memories and are addicted to information. They love to know and are voracious readers. They can quote things that they have read almost verbatim. They must guard against being elitists. They must also strive to balance their mental and physical selves and not become too cerebral thereby neglecting their bodies. Pronounced "aw-roon-mee-lah".

Countless other orisa exist. This is just a small list of some of the information compiled during my own study of Ifa. The descriptions above are metaphysical and not as anthropomorphic as most descriptions of the orisa. In an attempt to emphasize the spiritual, I purposely shied away from the more personified descriptions. Please bear in mind that the science or awo(mystery) of each orisa is EXTREMELY vast. As stated before each one of these forces has its own herbology, incantations, sacred stones, trees, metals et cetera dedicated to it. Each orisa could warrant a very lengthy volume or volumes of its own. The above descriptions are a mere introduction into this ancient knowledge. Although the list may assist you in figuring out which one of these forces of nature protects and guides you BEAR IN MIND that the only way to truly KNOW which orisa rules one's head is to have Difa (divination) performed by a competent priest or priestess.

Chapter Four
What is D'Ifa and What are Odu?

"One is never so comfortable or so
uncomfortable
That he is unable to D'Ifa"
Wholy Odu Odi

According to our Ancestors, to
D'Ifa is a fundamental component of
proper living. D'Ifa is a method of
accessing sacred memories that
have been recalled and preserved by
the Anago (Yoruba) for millennia.
These sacred memories are known
collectively and singularly as odu.
The memories are another form the
Olodumare takes as It diffuses in the
physical realm. Odu are the cosmic
wombs through which anything

must pass in order to exist. The odu also incarnated as Earthly beings.

Each odu contains countless verses and each verse recounts the remembrance of an event or an occurrence in what our Ancestors called "the land of beginnings". This is the time before recorded time. The remembrance of these events allows the client and the Awo (diviner/priest or priestess) to witness how this event was dealt with. A positive event exhibits how to properly praise and show gratitude towards the spirit realm. A negative event relays how problems can be solved and obstacles overcome. Each verse is replete with incantations, herbal prescriptions, and itans (anecdotal stories). Some verses also contain songs, rituals, prohibitions and prayers. Anything that is happening now has happened before; one needs only to consult Ifa to know how to handle things properly.

There are 16 principal odu; Ogbe, Oyeku, Iwori, Odi, Irosun, Oworin, Obara, Okanran, Ogunda, Osa, Ika, Oturupon, Otura, Irete, Ose, and Ofun. All odu exist in pairs, like parents, two are required to create one whole. Therefore the combination of 16 X 16 gives a total of 256 possible combinations of odu in all. Odu chronicles the lives of ancient humans and those creatures that existed in Aiye (the world) before man. Odu describes the way in which life as it is came to be.

Odu contains the memory of the Anago nation from the creation of the first eniyan (human) by Obatala. As stated above as the sacred container of the memory of the nation the corpus of Odu is a form of Olodumare. Odu is a force of nature, a selected head, an orisa. She is the womb in which we all exist; the "wombniverse", the sacred calabash that contains all things. She is often called the iyawo (bride) of Orunmila. Orunmila, as the Divine force of memory is the patron orisa of D'Ifa. Through Odu, D'Ifa provides us with access to the advice of the wisest and most ancient Ancestors. As the source through which we can access Odu, Orunmila himself is sometimes referred to as Ifa. (It is important to note here that the word "Ifa" is sometimes translated as "scraping together all of the world's wisdom".)

During a D'Ifa the Awo uses sacred objects to discern which sacred memory should be recounted in order to help the client. The applicable odu is then recited in the form of a poem, lyric verse, proverbs, itans (stories) or any mixture of these four. As the client listens, the Awo retells the centuries old tale and in this way is able to instruct the client. It is necessary to note that the Awo need not know the client's situation before determining which odu to recite. The Awo's communication with the Orisa into which he is initiated is all that is required. The Orisa communicates with the client's Ori and thereby reveals which odu is appropriate. The odu are oral scriptures and although many verses have been collected and written down the overwhelming majority remain recorded solely in the minds of adept initiates and their apprentices.

D'Ifa is an exact science not to be confused with channeling or fortune telling. The symbol that the sacred implements create when they are cast lets the Awo know which story to tell, which proverb to recite, which secret to reveal. The odu are an orally recorded history book and so the Awo does not act on clairvoyancy. It is the Ori of the client that ultimately guides the implements and makes its will known. D'Ifa is a way to make the will of the Ori known when one will not or cannot hear her own inner voice. Sometimes a D'Ifa is merely confirmation of something you have heard your inner voice saying all along. D'Ifa will let you know whether or not you are currently in alignment with your destiny and in the event that you are not the same D'Ifa will tell how to re-align yourself. Ifa practitioners D'Ifa for all major life events; marriage proposals, job offers, relocations et cetera.

In the West there are several written texts that have recorded odu. The most well known text containing odu is William Bascom's Sixteen Cowries. Bascom also produced another compilation of odu called Ifa Divination. These two texts exhibit the differences between the two forms of D'Ifa used in the system. The form used by babalawos and iyanifas (male and female initiates of Orunmila) is called Ifa and the form used by babalorisas (male initiates of any orisa other than Orunmila) and iyalorisas(female initiates of any orisa other than Orunmila) is called Merindilogun. Merindilogun is the Yoruba word for the number sixteen and denotes the number cowries used in this form of D'Ifa.

More recent publications include, Phillip Neimark and Afolabi Epega's Sacred Ifa Oracle and Maulana Karenga's Odu Ifa: The Ethical Teachings. The majority of odu quoted in Ona Agbani come from Sixteen Cowries or Odu Ifa. All of these books exhibit the beautiful choral poetry of the odu verses as well as the wealth of information amassed by our Ancestors. Karenga, Neimark and Epega also give brief explanations of each verse. The books all have the verses written in Yoruba and translated into English. In no way should these books or any written record be looked upon as the repository of all of the odu verses, Ifa is based upon oral history and so the vast majority of verses still remain only in the minds of adept priestesses and priests and their apprentices. However, the number of verses that one adept can memorize is astonishing and is exihibited in Sixteen Cowries. Baba Salako, a Babalorisa of Obatala, recited all of the verses represented in that text. Iba ara torun ("We pay homage to the citizens of Orun." A praise chant spoken when an Ancestor is mentioned.)

Chapter Five
How Do You Practice Ifa?
"That which made for the success of
those who
went before
Must be noted by those who come
after."

Wholy Odu Ogunda

Afrikan people currently find themselves (ourselves) in a global cultural identity crisis. The horrors of captivity, and the ravages of colonialism and neo-colonialism leave those of us who were victimized and/or re-located as a consequence of these conditions reluctant to embrace our origins. We all want to be anything other than Afrikan. We have adopted the white supremacist viewpoint of our colonizers and believe that anything Afrikan is backward, primitive and wicked. We internalize the labels given to us by our enslavers and call ourselves Jamaican, African American, Nigerian, Puerto Rican, Brazilian, and a host of other divisive titles. We no longer understand that wherever we are in the world we are ONE people with a common destiny and common characteristics. More disturbing is the current trend of identifying oneself with ONLY those areas of Afrika that have been deemed "civilized" by Western society. In accordance with this trend it is acceptable to be Ethiopian, Hebrew, Arabic, Asiatic, Nubian, or KMTic BUT sub-Saharan Afrika was/is the domain of polytheistic primitives who strayed from the path of righteousness. It seems that any area of Afrika having Quranic or Biblical import is advanced while all others remain backwards. This trend is yet another symptom of psychopathic racism and belief in a Eurocentric system which teaches that only the colonizer's "stamp of approval" makes a thing valid, acceptable and correct. Therefore, the first step towards practicing Ifa is to identify oneself as Afrikan first and then, if born in the America, Europe or the Caribbean due to the consequence of Maafa , West Afrikan in particular. This is not to add to the divisive ethnocentricity that is at the root of the mass genocide being committed in Afrika now. In accepting oneself as Afrikan, one must also accept the fact that ALL of Afrika shares a cultural unity, ALL of Afrika is interconnected. This is also not an act of denouncing the glorious empires of Kush, Ethiopia, KMT, or Nubia; nor the fact that the Afrikans who built those first three human civilizations are also the Ancestors of Afrikans born in the West and as such we can claim their achievements as our own. However, for the sake of our Ancestors who survived the horrors of the Middle Passage, persevered under the whip and the lash and still had enough faith in the Universe to give birth to us we MUST acknowledge that we are Yoruba, we are Mandinka, we are Wolof, we are Akom, we are Fon, we are Mende! WE ARE WEST AFRIKAN! We CANNOT let the suffering of our Ancestors be in vain, nor allow the greatness of their heritage to be lost and we most certainly MUST not arbitrarily GIVE IT AWAY! The historical fact is that 98% of all human cargo taken into captivity during the Maafa was taken from the West Coast of Afrika.

Our Ancestors were taken from areas largely unconnected with the origins of Judaism, Christianity or

Islam. The origins of these religions is beyond the shadow of a doubt Afrikan, but the places in which invading cultures stole Afrikan spirituality and transformed it into these religions are concentrated in East Afrika. Of course, by the time of the Maafa many West Afrikan communities had been ravaged by jihads from ruthless Arab invaders for centuries and were forced to either take shahadah (convert to Islam) or be killed. As a consequence, many captives arrived in the West as Muslims although it was very much mixed with indigenous beliefs. With these facts in mind it can be succinctly stated that the MAJORITY of Afrikans who were enslaved in the Western hemisphere (idiotically referred to as the "New World") practiced their own indigenous Afrikan, earth-centered, non-sexist, communalistic spiritual systems. We did not arrive on these shores as "blank slates" waiting to be written upon by our oppressors. To paraphrase the words of Ifa sage Bokonon Medahochi Kofi Zannu "Being in the West did not teach our Ancestors anything about God that they did not already know."

It is necessary to pause here and comment upon the "universality" of Ifa. According to the teachings of our Ancestors, the Supreme Being sent sages and prophets to each of the world's peoples to teach them how to live life properly. This is why Ifa does not proselytize, or try to convert others. Every group of people was gifted with methods of worship that are appropriate for them and it is arrogant and incorrect to assume that my way is correct for you. Each group of people is responsible for studying its ancestry and thereby determining which way of life is good for them to follow. Therefore it is best if Caucasians study the ancient Earth-based paths of their own ancestors and cease to usurp the ways of others. The danger in not following the ways of your ancestors is that you do not have a real understanding of the culture that begot these systems as so you must adapt the systems to your cultural mores and way of life and in doing so you ALWAYS do a disservice to that path. For example, earlier in this work I was forced to dispel the notion that the deity Obatala was white as in Caucasian, this is a notion that was stated as fact in a book by Philip Neimark a Caucasian practitioner of Ifa in his book The Way of the Orisa. In an attempt to "universal-ize" Ifa Mr. Neimark felt the need to claim that an ancient West Afrikan deity was Caucasian!

Your D.N.A. the genetic material you receive from your parents is part of what guides your understanding of the world. When met with a culture that is "foreign" to your experience and your genetic make-up you seek to filter it through your ways of thought and belief systems in order to understand it more fully. If you seek to implement parts of this doctrine you will do so within your own cultural parameters. Part of the current cultural ethos of the Caucasians is domination and so it is also general practice for them to set up their own methods of practicing a Native American, East Indian, Asian or Afrikan path and then proclaim themselves a chief or elder or high priest of this path and thereby become an acceptable authority on the belief systems of those people. This is the latest method of colonization and oppression. Although these self-styled Afrikan/Native American/Asian or Indian(Hindu) chiefs and priests claim to have evolved past racism, colonialism, and imperialism their actions are still guided by the Eurocentric psychopathic racist belief that people of color are not astute enough to represent our own belief systems! It also bypasses the fact that we are not obligated to share our ancient wisdom with others, it strips us of the luxury, freedom and safety of silence and exclusion! You cannot fully practice a spiritual system outside of the ramifications of the culture that begot that system. According to our Ancestors, what is right for one group of people in one place is NOT right for another group of people in another place. A Yoruba person would never try to convince one of his Fon neighbors who worships Vodun to worship the Orisa. No matter how much of a "melting pot" the West professes to be and how much rape and racial mixing took place before, during, and after the Maafa; Caucasians are not Afrikans, Asians, East Indians or Native Americans. Those who feel guilty for being a part of the race that has raped and pillaged all of the people of the Earth and is now on its way to destroying the very Earth itself should consult with their ancestors on the best course of action to assail this guilt and repay the ENORMOUS spiritual, financial, and emotional debts they owe the Universe. You cannot repay the spiritual debts accrued by your Ancestors by pretending that you are not the person who owes them!

It is best for people to respect the authority of their Ancestors by following the ways of those Ancestors. There are many beautiful, mysterious, Earth-based European paths; Wicce/Wicca, Celtic spirituality, Druidism, Fairy spirituality, and the Goddess path to name a few. Europeans should follow those paths and work to learn to TRULY respect the beliefs of others without having to dominate those systems in the process!

With that said, if one is truly interested in practicing Ifa she must begin with D'Ifa. Consult Ifa and receive the advice of the orisa and your Ancestors. Consult a well-known Awo(priest or priestess) in your area. Generally if you ask around at Black bookstores or cultural arts centers (like Afrikan dance and drum studios) you will find that they know someone. PLEASE only utilize Awo that come highly recommended, if someone tells you they had a bad experience with an Awo go to a different priestess or priest. Remember that those who practice Ifa are to maintain an unblemished reputation. If your search for a competent Awo is unsuccessful you may contact the author by email

(Got2BOshun@msn.com) and receive a D'Ifa this way. BE ADVISED that it is always BEST to receive D'Ifa in person! This is the ancient way; the way our Ancestors did it! However, the procedure can be modified for extenuating circumstances. Ifa is dynamic not static.

D'Ifa will inform you of your personal dietary taboos, and rules of conduct. You will be told which orisa rules your head and how that impacts your life. You will receive the odu that is active in your life right now and be given ebos(sacrifices) to do if necessary in order to place yourself in alignment with your destiny. A D'Ifa will let you know whether you are currently in Ire; which is the state of being in alignment with your destiny or Ibi/Osogbo; which is the state in which there is an obstacle in your path. Ebos may involve setting up shrines to particular deities, preparing and presenting foods to particular deities, giving offerings to a particular deity, or personal meditation, rest, and prayer. Whenever one is asked through D'Ifa to give an ebo it is important to remember that the ebo is a physical reminder of a transformation that is needed. If one does not change the behavior then the ebo was done in vain. An ebo is not the cure to the problem. An ebo is an indication to the Universe that you are ready to begin to work on the issue and you are asking for the support of the Divine in your efforts.

Any personal questions that you have can be asked of the Orisa as well. Further clarity on your odu, your orisa or anything that you did not understand should also be offered as part of your D'Ifa. Some communities refer to D'Ifa as Dafa or divination or simply as "having a reading". Do not be put off as they all mean the same thing. D'Ifa is the most ancient method of referring to this communion with the Divine.

After D'Ifa, those who are still serious about practicing Ifa should set up an Ojubo Egun, an Ancestral Shrine. The Ancestral Shrine is the first of many sacred spaces devotees create in their homes. The Ancestral Shrine is the point of contact between the devotee and her bloodline Ancestors. (If you were adopted PLEASE feel free to use the bloodline of your adoptive family as they obviously agreed in Orun before you were born to make you a part of their lineage. You may also use those ancestors of your biological family if you know them.) Ifa is a path of aligning yourself with the spirit realm and the place to begin this alignment is at home, with your family, your Ancestors. Your Ancestors are not "ghosts" or "spooks" or "haints"; they loved and cared for you in life and they wish to do the same from the Spirit Realm. Your Ancestors have a vested interest in your life because according to Ifa "If my mother gave birth to be in full, I will in turn give birth to her" therefore our Egun want to see us do well in life so that they can be re-born into happy homes and because they LOVE us! Ifa teaches us in the odu Irosun that our Ancestors wait outside the gates of our lives until we invite them in. The odu goes on to say that they want to grant all of our righteous requests if we but ask. Introduction to the practices of Ifa must begin with the Ancestral Shrine because the family deceased are the closest spiritual connection for any human being.

Ojubo Egun

Low table or box covered with white cloth or it may sit on the floor
1 large glass of water or 9 small glasses
9 pennies
a piece of cloth
a list of names of all RIGHTEOUS ancestors
photographs of righteous ancestors (NO LIVING PEOPLE IN PHOTOGRAPHS!!!!!)
tobacco
1 large white candle or 9 small white candles
items belonging to deceased family members (NO ITEMS FROM PEOPLE WHO ARE LIVING!!!!!!!!)
The Ancestral Shrine is an area ruled by the Orisa Oya as she is the Mother of the Ancestral

Realm. As such, there is much usage of the number nine and the metal copper on this shrine.

Your Ancestral Shrine may be as simple or as elaborate as you desire. The only items strictly required from the list above are the names of your righteous ancestors, the white candle and the water. But keep in mind that your shrine is your offering to your family Ancestors, so you will get what you give. The shrine informs your Ancestors that you remember and acknowledge their Divine presence. It expresses your desire to include your Ancestors in your life. Ancestral communion is recognition of the fact that "spirit does not die" . The spirit of your Grandmother for example loves and protects you in death just as she always loved and protected you in life. How rude it would be to ignore her presence simply because it is in a different form! How ignorant it would be not to continue to seek her wisdom! Your shrine is proof that you know your Ancestors are here and that you want their guidance. You may request that your Ancestors do not manifest themselves in ways that will frighten you. To scare their offspring is not the wish of the Ancestors. Did they ever delight in frightening you when they were living? Ancestors do not develop a love for scaring family members because they enter the spirit realm. Your Ancestors are your family and they only wish what is best for you, deal with them from that perspective.

In order to activate your ancestral altar and re-open your spiritual self to the Spiritual Realm you must go before your shrine for nine days at the same time each day. Dawn, dusk, or midnight are the best times for spiritual communion. However, if these times do not fit into your schedule, find a time when you can sit undisturbed and listen for the voices of your predecessors. I prefer to leave the candle on my shrine burning at all times, however, if you have put your candle out re-light it to open your ritual. Use the following invocation for the spirits of your family Egun:

Egun mojuba o
Mojuba o
Mojuba YeYe
Mojuba BaBa
Mojuba gbogbo egun idile mi
nbelese Olodumare ibaye Orun
Ibaye torun
Iba awon YeYe tonu
Iba awon BaBa tonu
Iba ara torun
Iba a se name of each righteous ancestor

Add your own personal prayer
Ase Ase Ase

Pronunciation of prayer
Mohjoobah   bohgboh   ehgoon
eedehlehmee   inbehlehse
Ohlohdoomahray eebahyah Ohroon
Eebahyah tohroon
Eebah ahwan Yayay tohnoo
Eebah Bahbah tohnoo
Eebah ahrah tohroon
Eebah   ah   shay   name   of   each
righteous ancestor
Add   your   own   personal   prayer   to
your ancestors
Ahshay Ahshay Ahshay

Translation of prayer

Ancestors I pay homage to you oh
I pay homage oh
I pay homage to the Mothers
I pay homage to the Fathers
I pay homage to all of the righteous
ancestors of my family lineage who

now bow at the feet of Olodumare in Orun
We pay homage to Orun
We pay homage to the Mothers that were lost
We pay homage to the Fathers that were lost
We pay homage to the citizens of Orun
We pay homage to name of each righteous ancestor
Add your own personal prayer
It is so, it is so, it is so

The calling of the name of each of the righteous Ancestors is PARAMOUNT in the rite of Egun worship. When one's name ceases to be called by one's progeny she ceases to be and Egun and moves into another realm. This realm is the being of Damballah Wedo the totality of all those Ancestors whose names have been forgotten. This realm is more difficult to access. It is the responsibility of the living family members to maintain contact with the family members in Orun. As Julia Dash so eloquently states through the words of Eula in "Daughters of the Dust";"...we the bridge what they cross over on, we the tie between then and now, between the past and the story what'a come..." If we are to create healthy families and reconstruct the glory of our Afrikan past we MUST communicate with our Ancestors! In ancient times hundreds of years would pass before a spirit would move into the realm of Damballah Wedo, now we allow it to happen even in our own lifetimes. When is the last time you called the name of your Great Grandmother or remembered her deeds? Call upon the names of your Ancestors and watch them set your feet on the path towards righteousness.

Once you have activated your shrine in this way it is established as the "seat" of your Egun in your home. Go before it every day. After the initial nine days you may go before it any time, but find some way of revering you Egun daily. THE single most important way to worship your Egun is through your actions. The Egun are the moral guide of the community. As such you should allow them to guide your actions. If there is something that you would not do in front of your Grandfather for example, then you know that that is something that you should not do at all. Remember that your elders are always with you in their spirit form; just because you cannot see them does not mean they are not there. ACT ACCORDINGLY!

One of the many unfortunate consequences of the Maafa is that the position of Egun in Ifa was distorted. Many practitioners of Ifa use the term "egun" to denote unelevated ancestral spirits who cause harm or bring confusion to those in the Earthly realms. While unelevated spiritual beings do exist the Yoruba word Egun means "bones" and refers to any deceased family member and not just unelevated ones. Egun reverence is also associated with the Palo sect of Ifa. Palo deals almost exclusively with Egun awo (mysteries/magick). Because some Paleros (palo priests and priestesses) have used this power to do negative deeds the entire sect is generally dismissed as the "left hand path" or a part of Ifa devoted to promoting negativity. However, anything that is balanced has both a left and a right, both positive and negative and both sides are necessary. Palo (also called Palo Mayombe) is a mixture of Ifa from the Anago people of Nigeria and Nganga from the people of the

Kongo. It is a Western form of Ifa that should not be considered the "dark side" of Ifa.

Among other Ifa adherents Egun reverence and even the Egungun priesthood is seen as being lower than orisa reverence and the orisa priesthood. While a hierarchy did exist in ancient time our Ancestors overstood that Egun worship is the foundation of any spiritual undertaking.

Overstanding that your Ancestors are Divine is essential to realizing that you are Divine. Once you recognize yourself as a Divine vessel of the Most High it is easier for you to move towards becoming Wholy or accepting your role as a portion of the Whole, the Wombniverse, the ALL. This cannot be achieved if you believe yourself to be a mortal being only. Hence, anyone who is re-introducing their spirit to Ifa MUST begin with their own family EGUN!

Once you have prayed and meditated with your Egun for a minimum of 21 days(that is 12 in addition to the original 9 days during which you opened the shrine) you should have formed a relationship with them and should begin to be able to see the subtle ways in which they interact with you in your daily life. It will take some people longer than 21 days but it will probably not take anyone less than 21 days as that is generally how long it takes one to become attuned to anything. After this initial period of reconnection with your Egun you may create spaces for deceased Afrikan heroes in your home. You may wish to create an actual shrine or you may choose to simply have pictures of these leaders hanging throughout your home. Select only those whose vibrations you wish to have in your space.

Also after that initial 21 days you should begin to cultivate relationship with your highest self, your Ori. Your Ori is the animating force of your physical body in this particular lifetime. Ori is your own personal spiritual force. It was your ori that guided the formation of your body in the womb of your mother. It was your ori that told you to take your first steps and to attempt your first words. Your ori is that portion of Olodumare that lives within you. Just as they were the gateway into this physical life by providing you with a family to be born into, the Ancestors are the gateway to your spiritual life as well. Once you walked through that first spiritual gateway you are prepared to move through the next one.

Each stage of devoting oneself to Ifa is marked by a ritual to open up your spiritual, emotional, and physical selves to the realities of the

Wombniverse. As such, one can receive consecrated sacred implements with which to communicate with her Ancestors. This is generally referred to as "receiving your Ancestor Pots". However, your DNA grants you the psychic and spiritual ability to communicate with your Ancestors from the moment that you are born. Therefore, most individuals can benefit from creating a relationship with their Egun before moving on to receive the sacred implements that will strengthen that relationship. Considering our current spiritual state, it is of the utmost importance that we regain our spiritual sense of self and not lean on rituals or priests and priestesses as our connections to the spirit realm. We should not trade one spiritual master for another; we must become the captains of our own spiritual fates. Each person must take full responsibility for her own spiritual growth and development. One can also be initiated as an Egungun priest or priestess and become a conduit between the physical realm and the realm of the Ancestors. Egungun priests and priestess deal specifically with ancestral concerns and make sure the lines of communication between the living and the dead remain open. It is Egungun initiates who prepare the Ancestral pots. Egungun priests and priestess are part of the Egungun society whose functions and duties are awo(unknown to the uninitiated).

The second stage of practicing Ifa is the cultivation and maintainance of a relationship with your ori. Your ori is the repository of your ase. All of your physical, mental and spiritual powers originate in you ori. Our Ancestors taught us to revere Ori daily at dawn in order to "break the kola nut of ase" or to receive the mystical powers of the Universe. We are taught that when we bow to pay homage to our Ori on Earth, our Iponri (all of the Ori we have had in previous incarnations and all of the Ori we will have in the future) bows before Olodumare in Orun.

First, set up an ori shrine. Set up a shrine to you. Let it reflect all you know yourself to be and all that you wish to become. Let the pictures be pictures of you in an enlightened state, pictures when you could feel your Highest Self manifesting, when you experienced your God or Goddess essence. Place items on it that speak to who you are and who you will be in the future. Place the shrine in a high place so that you will be reminded to act in an elevated way or place it on the ground if you need to re-establish your foundation. Use colors and numbers that are significant to you.

Once you have established an ori shrine. Go before it for 8 days consecutively at dawn. The number eight is the number used when working with Ori because it is the number of Obatala and the area of the body he rules is the head. Check your local weather listings or almanac to see what time the sun rises in your area. Prostrate yourself before you Highest Self and recite the following iwure (prayer).

Ori nikan lo to alasan barokun
Bi mo ba lowo lowo
Ori ni oro fun
Ori mi iwo ni
Bi mo ba timo laiye
Ori ni oro fun
Ori mi iwo ni
Ire gbogbo timo laiye
Ori ni oro fun
Ori mi iwo ni

Pronunciation of prayer

Ohree   neekahn   lohtohalahsan
bahrohkoon
Bee moh bah lohwoh lohwoh
Ohree nee ohrohfoon
Ohree mee eewoh nee
Bee moh bah teemoh lahyay
Ohree nee ohrohfoon
Ohree mee eewohnee
Eeeray bohgboh teemoh lahyay
Ohree nee ohrohfoon
Ohree mee eewoh nee

Ahshay ahshay ahshay

Translation of prayer
It is Ori alone who can accompany
his devotee on a distant journey to
any place without turning back
If I have money it is Ori I will praise
My Ori it is you
If I have children it is Ori to whom I
will give the praise
My Ori it is you

All good things that I have on Earth
it is Ori to whom I will give the
praise
My Ori it is you

It is so, it is so, it is so

Our Ancestors taught that in
times of distress and trouble our
mother or father orisa may not be
accessible. We have fallen out of
touch with these deities, hence the
distress. Therefore they admonished
us to place the worship of Ori above
all others. Venerate and exalt your
Ori daily in order to re-construct
your ability to listen to this inner
voice. Your Ori is the home of your
destiny in this lifetime, if you are to
fulfill that destiny you must be
guided by Ori.

The rite that marks the receipt of
the sacred implements of Ori is
performed when one reaches the
age of seven. It is called the Onifa

rite or the "hand of Ifa". This establishes the child as a member of the community and as a spirit who has chosen to remain the physical realm. At this time the child is no longer a baby and is held responsible for his actions by his parents and the community in which he lives. In these modern times, when we no longer have the luxury of being born into the culture and find ourselves in the odd position of having to "convert" to it, it is necessary to perform this ritual on adults as well.

If you are fortunate enough to affiliate yourself with a community of Ifa devotees, you will sooner or later be faced with the decision of whether or not to ritualistically devote yourself to Ifa as a way of life. This practice is known as "receiving your ilekes". The ilekes are beaded necklaces worn by devotees for protection and identification. The word ileke simply means "beads". Generally in the West each devotee receives a set of five necklaces. Each necklace represents an orisa. The five ileke that are usually given belong to Sango, Osun, Yemonja, Obatala and Esu/Elegba. The decision to receive your ilekes should of course be placed before your Ancestors and Ifa during a D'Ifa and you should meditate carefully upon when would be the right time for you to undergo this ancient rite.

The wearing of five necklaces is peculiar to the Western hemisphere and is a practice our Ancestors created in order to insure that a small portion of the awo of each orisa was given to each devotee. Although the ancient practice had been to let the majority of the mystic knowledge lie in the hands of the clergy of the tradition, after the Maafa we could no longer afford such a luxury. Therefore, we ceased to give one ileke to specified people and gave many to all.

Another important rite is the "receiving of the warriors". In this ritual, the devotee receives the sacred implements of Ogun, Esu, Osoosi and sometimes Osun (not to be confused with Oshun). These orisa will fight your battles for you as it is spiritually, physically, and emotionally detrimental for you to harbor aggression.

As a spiritual system, the goal of Ifa is the development of the spirit. Therefore it is replete with rites that make us more open to the spiritual realms. This is the goal of the rites mentioned above and all of the other rituals associated with the tradition. In short, the goal is transformation; to create TRUE human beings those who act according to their connection to the Universe, to live with Iwa Pele.

Through Ifa we learn never to forget that our essence, our Highest Self, our True Self is spiritual.

The culmination of these rites is initiation into orisa. This rite makes one a vessel of the power of that orisa. As an initiated Ol'orisa (orisa priest or priestess) one is responsible for reminding others of the God or Goddess that dwells within. The duties of each Ol'orisa vary depending upon why he was initiated. However, some things that they may do are perform divinations, teach songs and incantations, study odu, lead egbes, lead bembes, give ilekes, give warriors, perform Onifa (only those initiated into Orunmila), officiate at esentaiyes (naming ceremonies) and igbeyawos (weddings), initiate others into orisa and basically handle the spiritual needs of the community. Every individual is not destined for the priesthood and usually Difa reveals who is to be dedicated to orisa in this way.

The methods in which rituals are performed in Ifa are awo. They are not known by the uninitiated. Many books on the market boast that they are written by authentic practitioners who have revealed all of the secrets of initiations. Rest assured, if one is truly an authentic practitioner he or she would NOT under any circumstances reveal those things which are awo. In the words of our Ancestors, "those who know don't tell and those who tell don't know."

Yoruba Pronunciation Key

The Yoruba language has its own lettering system and form of pronunciation. Yoruba is also a tonal language that utilizes the tones referred to in Western musical terminology as do, re, mi. Do is a high tone, re is a mid-tone, and mi is a low tone. I will not attempt to teach to tonality of the language as that is best undertaken by one for whom Yoruba is her mother tongue. However here is a listing of the Yoruba letters and the sounds each one makes to assist the reader in saying the prayers correctly. Remember this is one of the languages of your Ancestors and even if your mouth does not recall

the words and sounds, your Ori,
your soul remembers!

A   ah as in adept
B   b as in boy

D   d as in dog
E   eh as in egg
F   f as in fat
G   g as in good
GB g with a guttural b behind it
H   h as in how
I   ee as in bee
J   j as in joy
K   k as in kiss
L   l as in love
M   m as in me
N   n as in no
O   oh as in open
O   aw as in awful
P   kp the k as in kiss sound with a
p sound after
R   r as in row
S   s as in see
S   sh as in she

T t as in toy
U ooh as in tool
V v as in very
W w as in wet
Y y as in yet

Chapter Six

What is an Egbe and Why is it Necessary?

"Orunmila says there should be a
gathering
together like trees do to form a
forest...
Ifa says we should gather together
and not walk alone"
Wholy Odu Oyeku Meji

The nature of Olodumare's
Universe is communal. Therefore,
one cannot truly benefit from the

practices of Ifa without the vital component of communal living, the community itself. Ifa is a way of life, a method of conducting oneself, a way of moving through the world. Your resolve to live Ifa will be strengthened by surrounding yourself with a community of believers. If no such community exists where you are, surround yourself with your Ancestors and Orisa and ask them to place you within such a community. To truly live Ifa one must sing the songs, perform the dances and participate in the rituals that align her with the unseen realm; all of these practices require a community.

Seeing this necessity, our Ancestors created societies to maintain and further the cause of Ifa from the moment their Afrikan feet touched Western soil. These societies were and are called peristyles, houses, iles, voodoos, kilombos and egbes. Egbe is the Yoruba word for society. In ancient times, an Egbe was a group of people devoted to any specific cause. There was an egbe of market women, an egbe of individuals born in the same year, and many others. Among these were also the egbes devoted to the worship of a particular orisa. People who had received special favors from a certain orisa or who were chosen by a particular orisa joined these egbes in order to learn the awo (mysteries/ magick) of that orisa.

In modern times, an Egbe is generally a community of people who practice Ifa. Although some extremely large Ifa communities still divide themselves into smaller egbes according to the orisa that rules one head. Ifa communities may also still be called houses or iles. Each egbe is guided by a priest or priestess and sometimes both. Generally, the

Egbe is named after the orisa that the head priest/ess is initiated into. An egbe may be called Egbe Osun, Egbe Ogun et cetera.

Within an egbe one will learn the songs, dances and rituals that are the life's blood of Ifa. As a distinctly Afrikan spiritual system Ifa celebrates life through dance, song, poetry and oral history. These are the elements that kept Ifa and our Ancestors alive during the Maafa. These are quintessential parts of Afrikan culture and heritage. They also teach moral lessons and transmit the ethos, the way of being, to the children. From an Afrikan perspective, life is art and art is one of the highest expressions of human life.

Because Ifa is not an organized religion, each egbe has its own style. Though many meet on Sunday to accommodate the work schedules of the members, some meet every four days following the ancient Yoruba calendar of a four day week. Most, but not all, require that white is worn during meetings and rituals as this is the ancient ritual uniform. Some meet only to do rituals or have bembes (spiritual festivals) for the orisa, while others see each other often and share a bond similar to that of an extended family.

One thing that each egbe does provide is an opportunity for its members to immerse themselves in West Afrikan culture. Your egbe should be your haven from the outside world, your shelter from the shitstem of Babylon. Within its walls (figuratively or actually) you should feel protected and surrounded by the orisa and your Ancestors. Each member should do his best not to bring the pettiness, the jealousy, the greed or the wickedness of the Western world into the Afrikan reality of the Egbe. The vibration of the egbe is not the responsibility of the guiding priest or priestess but of the members themselves. Once again each individual must take responsibility for her own actions, growth and development.

It is also the responsibility of each devotee of Ifa to participate in the global egbe of Ifa by respecting and acknowledging other practitioners of this way of life. Do not allow yourself to be pulled into the slave mentality of judging one form of Ifa to be better than or purer than another. From the west coast of Afrika to the shores of the Americas and the islands of the Caribbean we were all polluted by the Western mentality that attempted to turn us into chattel. There is no form of Ifa that remains untainted by the stain of the Maafa. Even Ile Ife, Nigeria; the place our Ancestors called the "land where the day first dawned" and therefore the birthplace of Ifa and sacred city of Orunmila; is more devoted in this day and time to regurgitating the dogma of Christianity than espousing the wisdom of Orunmila. When I visited Nigeria in 1999, I was greatly disappointed to see that the sacred groves of the Orisa and Ancestral mothers and fathers were in extreme disrepair. A prime example was the grove which houses the staff of Warrior Ancestor Oranmiyan (Iba ara torun). Oranmiyan is a Yoruba warrior hero who sunk into the Earth upon his death and stated that if the Yoruba people every needed him all they had to do was tap the ground beside his staff (an ancient obelisk) and he would rise and fight for them. This grove was covered in trash, and there were pigs rooting around in it! My entire stay in Nigeria made it clear to me that all over the globe we have been wounded by the Maafa but the visit to Oranmiyan's grove was the definitive moment!

As Afrikans, we are struggling all over the globe to regain those parts of ourselves that were torn from us as a consequence of colonialism. As such, we must see the differences in our ways of practicing Ifa as ecological necessities due to the circumstances our Ancestors found themselves in. Did the Yoruba captive see himself as different if he was taken to Haiti instead of Cuba? History suggests not. Were you more Yoruba than me because your colonizer forced you to speak Portuguese and while mine beat English into my tongue? Our shared culture says no. Then we cannot continue to argue that Santeria is better than Lukumi or Voodoo more sacred than Sango Baptiste. We cannot say that one is not truly initiated unless his or her spiritual leaders are from Nigeria or Cuba or

Brazil. This is essentially an argument over who had the best oppressor! When we compartmentalize the tradition in this way we are saying "My massa was better than yours!" If we look at this huge controversy from the perspective of our Ancestors, those who are responsible for creating these Western forms of Ifa, it is clear that they could not have seen slavery in one place as being better or worse than slavery in another place! Our Ancestors created these Western forms of Ifa to achieve the goal of having no slavery at all! (In which they succeeded!) The differences in the forms are by necessity not by design!

Chapter Seven
What is the Role of Women in Ifa?

"You will be their mother forever
You will also sustain the world..."
Wholy Odu Osa Meji

Western society is patriarchal. Patriarchal is used here to denote not only a society that is ruled by men, but also a society in which male supremacy is condoned, encouraged and cultivated. Patriarchal societies are those in which men (in the case of Western society white men) are the focal point and women and children are relegated to the status of second class citizens whose needs, wants and desires are not as important as the needs, wants, and desires of men. As such those socialized within any Western society have a tendency to adopt a patriarchal world view as well. Oftentimes, when we re-claim ways of living that differ from what we are used to we will bring our old perspectives and views with us. Thus, while neither pre-colonial West Afrika nor the spiritual systems therein were patriarchal; Ifa is sometimes viewed and practiced as a patriarchal system. According to the teachings of our Ancestors this is a dangerous and most serious error.

Our Ancestors taught that it was nonsensical and dangerous to relegate women, and the feminine aspects of the Divine to the background. For the sustainer of our very existence is feminine. Odu is the womb in which all things exist. She is the calabash that holds all things seen and unseen. She is the Wombniverse. As such, if her power is not respected and duly revered all things, all life will cease to be.

So speaks the Wholy Odu Osa Meji:

"D'Ifa was performed for Odu, Obarisa, and Ogun,
When they were coming from Orun to Aiye...
To make the world so that the world would be good.
Odu said: 'O Olodumare...what is my power?'
Olodumare said: 'you will be their mother forever. And you will also sustain the world.'
It was then that Olodumare gave women the power and authority so that anything men wished to do,
They could dare not do it successfully without women.
Odu said that everything that people would want to do,

If they do not include women,
It would not be possible.
Obarisa said that people should always respect women greatly. For if they always respect women greatly, the world will be in right order."

This odu makes it quite clear that Olodumare decreed when Aiye was being created that women should participate in all earthly activities both large and small if we wish these activities to succeed. If women are not included and "respected greatly" the things we are trying to accomplish will "not be possible". This ancient teaching is often overlooked within the inner workings of the various temples, iles, and egbes that claim to be practicing Ifa. From Nigeria to the Americas there are many houses treat women with the same misogynistic attitudes that are the foundation of Judaism, Christianity and Islam. Women are relegated to the position of cooks, shrine decorators, singers, and basic support; while the true work of running the temple rests within the hands of men. The American and Caribbean houses purport that this way must be correct as it is the way it is generally done in Nigeria. However, Nigeria has fallen victim to the same Western psychosexual maladjustments that its British oppressors suffered from. Nigeria too has ceased to listen to voices of the Ancestors as heard in Osa Meji. According to Ifa, women are to be active participants in all levels of society if we wish that society to be successful and balanced.

Unfortunately, women raised within Western societies have a tendency to support the misogynistic treatment that they receive. Women will internalize and therefore act upon the view that they are the weaker, less intelligent and inferior gender. We as women do not expect to see other women in positions of authority and therefore do not question it if we do not see it. Or if, as is the case with the Egbe I co-founded, there is a male and female head; women will assume just as often as men do that the male is the most knowledgeable of the two leaders and will treat the woman as if she is merely the "help meet" of the man. We have also been socialized to accept physical, emotional, and verbal abuse from men as a normal way of being and therefore we do not protect ourselves or our sistren when we see or experience these atrocious acts being committed. The saddest and most horrible crime is when we are told that patriarchal attitudes and ways of acting are AFRIKAN and that we are being UN-AFRIKAN if we speak out against them!

Sistahs, as physical manifestations of the cosmological power of Odu we are the repositories of ase. There is not one ritual in Ifa that can be performed properly without a woman being present! We hold ase within our wombs! We must re-member this fact and carry ourselves accordingly. We are not(as Zora Neale Hurston so aptly stated in her treatise on Afrikan spirituality in Haiti and Jamaiaca Tell My Horse)"the mules of the world" so we should cease to act as if we are and refuse to allow ourselves to be treated as such! It is our collective ase that sustains the Universe! Removal of the feminine ase results in death, and destruction.

Wholy Odu Ose'Tura teaches:

"D'Ifa was performed for the 200 Irunmole(Forces of Light who are the progenitors of the orisa) on the right side of Olodumare

And the same was done for the 200 Irunmole on the left side of Olodumare

They came to Aiye with Osun, the elegant one, owner of the beautiful coral comb,

In order to prepare the world for all creatures.

When they got to Aiye the 400 male Irunmole told Osun that her job was to cook their food and they proceeded to go about the work of creating the Aiye.

They had been instructed to build a grove(an outdoor temple),clear the land for a farm and build a road

Osun offered suggestions as to how this work should be completed

But the male deities told her to return to her cooking

Osun took her complaint to
Olodumare
Olodumare told her that whatever
recourse she felt was appropriate
Olodumare would grant her the ASE
to do it
The 400 Irunmole cleared the land
for the grove and went to rest,
When they returned it was
overgrown
They cleared a path through the
forest to make a road and went to
sleep for the night
The next morning the road was once
again impassable
They removed the trees and stumps
in order to plow the land to grow
food and went to eat
When they back it appeared as if no
work had been done
And on and on it went
Until finally the 400 Irunmole
decided this task was impossible
They went to Olodumare and said
that it could not be done

This work of creating Aiye was too difficult
Olodumare asked 'What about Osun, the only woman among you,'
'Did you ask her advice, did you give her due respect?'
The 400 Irunmole confessed that they had shunned Osun's advice and given her the duty of cooking
Olodumare sent them back to Aiye to ask the forgiveness of Osun
When they returned to Aiye
Osun explained that since she was not considered worthy to be a part of the work of creating Aiye She had removed her ase from their endeavors and that she had no intention of returning it
BUT if she became pregnant and gave birth to a male divinity
That divinity would allow her ase to return to Aiye again
She said that each Irunmole was to give her some of his ase by placing his hand on her Ori

And through this ase she would conceive

They should then pray that the child would be male because if it were not she would NOT lend her ase to Aiye ever again

The male Irunmole granted Osun's wish and prayed fervently for nine months for the birth of a male child

Osun delivered alone and one the appointed day emerged from her birthing chamber announcing that the child's name was

Esu Odara

And that HE would allow her ase to once again be a part of Aiye

Thus we always give due respect to Osun

The unseen mother who is present at every gathering."

This then is the true role of the Afrikan woman and the woman in Ifa. Ifa cosmology recognizes each woman as one who carries the power to mother. We are the carriers, the keepers and the caretakers of the ase. We are the repository of the Power that makes things happen. We hold within us the Power of the Wombniverse. This truth does not in any way diminish the necessity of men, nor is it a statement of female superiority. Oyeronke Oyewumi,a Yoruba woman born and raised in Nigeria describes it this way:

"Motherhood occupies a special place in African cultures and societies. mothers are the essential building block of social relationships, identities, and indeed society. Because mothers symbolize familial ties, unconditional love and loyalty, motherhood is invoked even in extrafamiliial situations that calls upon these values. For example, in the Ogboni a traditional political organization which formed part of the hierarchy of governance in some Yoruba polities, members refer to each other as omoya - mother's child— emphasizing that fraternal and sororal bonds derive from mother and the institution of motherhood (Oyewumi 2003a). At the moment of birth, two entities are born - a baby and a mother. In Yoruba language, the term for mother is abiyamo, which can be translated as natal mother or nursing mother. In everyday usage, the term abiyamo is usually accompanied by another one ikunle which means kneeling, the preferred birthing position in the culture. Thus ikunle abiyamo refers to the kneeling of a mother in labor. The day a particular mother gives birth is referred to as ojo ikunle (day of birth). The kneeling posture is invested with a lot of meaning, as is demonstrated by the prevalence of this pose in Yoruba art. In the cosmology, Ikunle recalls akunleyan - the pregestation act of kneeling before the Creator to choose one's - ori— Destiny on earth. It is significant that the most fateful choice any individual makes at this crucial pre-earthly moment is the selection of one's mother. Growing up in Yorubaland, one learns to respect the potency of the mother's words because children are told that the only person whose curse has no antidote is one's mother's curse. Children know that mothers have a special ase to which they routinely draw attention by invoking ikunle abiyamo —-birth processes and the mystical and social values associated with them. Centering African experiences of motherhood reveals that motherhood is not merely an earthly institution: it is pregestational, presocial, prenatal, postnatal, and lifelong. Precisely because there are no male equivalents of motherly responsibilities, motherhood transcends gender. Fatherhood is not its equivalent. As I have written elsewhere, mothers are not merely women. One cannot overemphasize the notion of pregestational motherhood; its immediate impact is to deepen temporally, and widen spatially the scope of the institution. The Yoruba world consists of the unborn, the living, and the dead, and motherhood is present in all these realms. Consequently, because the whole community is naturally invested in it there is no greater public institution than motherhood."

If we choose to allow our ase to be used by those who do not give us the respect we are due then we have only ourselves to blame. If we find ourselves in a situation in which we are not being respected we have only to remove our ase totally from it and it will fail. Remove your ase from such situations by refusing to give them any thought, any time, any attention; refuse to give them any of your energy. We are not powerless or voiceless. Olodumare will stand with us as she stood with Osun!

Ifa is a system that values balance above all else. If women are being mistreated and oppressed there is no balance. Thus men and women are reminded in Wholy Odu Osa Meji to:

"Bend your knee (kneel) to woman
It is woman who brought you into this world
It is woman who recognized you
Before you came to be recognized as a human being
Bend your knee to woman,o!"

Chapter Eight

What is our purpose in life and How do we achieve this purpose?

"Surely, humans have been chosen
to bring good into the world..."
Wholy Odu Irosu'Wori

As stated in earlier chapters, the ancient Yoruba word for human being is eniyan. Eniyan is translated as "chosen one". Once Olodumare grants the ase that makes your conception a reality, you are chosen. And as the above odu states, there is no doubt what you are chosen for.

In the Western world, the question "why am I here" is often asked of religious teachers, scholars and sages. Ifa answers this question succinctly in a verse of the Wholy Odu Irosu'Wori.

"Surely, humans have been chosen to bring good into the world.
Morantan(the priest's name means 'the all knowing one'), priest of Orunmila, performed a D'Ifa for Orunmila
He told Orunmila that the people of the world would come to ask him a certain question.
And as the D'Ifa prophesied it came to pass...
The people said: 'Going back and forth to Aiye tires us Orunmila. Therefore, please allow us to rest in Orun.'
Orunmila said: 'You cannot avoid going back and forth to Aiye,

Until you bring about the good condition that Olodumare has ordained for every human being.
After then, you may rest in Orun.'
They asked 'What is the good condition?'
Orunmila said: 'The good condition is a good world:
A world in which there is full knowledge of all things;
Happiness everywhere;
Life without anxiety or fear of enemies;
Without clashes with dangerous animals;
Without fear of death, disease, litigation, losses, or sorcery;
Without fear of injury from water or fire; and
Without fear of poverty or misery.
Because of your wisdom, your compelling desire for Iwa Pele (good character) and your internal strength.

The things needed to bring about the good condition in the world then are:

Wisdom that is fully adequate to govern the world;

Ebo (sacrifice); iwa (character); the love of doing good for all people, especially those who are in need,

And those who seek assistance from us;

And the eagerness and struggle to increase good in the world,

And not let any good at all be lost.

People will continue to go to Orun;

And they will go back and forth to Aiye after their transfiguration,

Until everyone has achieved the good condition.

Thus when the children of Oduduwa[progenitor of the Yoruba people whose name means 'the Black one comes'] gather together,

Those chosen to bring good into the world are called eniyan or chosen ones."

There is no doubt as to why we are here or why we were born. There is no doubt as to whether or not we were meant to be born. Each and every child conceived is a "chosen one", handpicked by Olodumare to assist in the great work of bringing about the "good condition". If you are devoting your life to Ifa, then you are consciously devoting your life to this mission. Those who are not devoted to Ifa are also a part of this mission even though they are ignorant of it.

This odu is also very specific as to who was chosen and why. "The children of Oduduwa" is a reference to the offspring of the progenitor of the Yoruba people. The Biblical Adam is the Hebrew equivalent to Oduduwa. Oduduwa is the first eniyan. Oduduwa is also known as Odua(which translates as 'the womb comes') in certain circles and is said to have been female. Within the Yoruba language there are no gender specific pronouns, no he or she, therefore it is difficult to determine the gender of this Ancestor. It is extremely important to note that all scientific evidence suggests that our oldest Ancestor was an Afrikan female.

Why were the children of Oduduwa chosen to bring good into the world? The odu tells us it is "because of your wisdom, your compelling desire for Iwa Pele(gentle character), and your internal strength...". We the ones best suited for the job. Wonder at who and what you are no longer. Set forth immediately to do the work that you were sent here to do!

Once your purpose in life has been identified the next intelligent query would be how to fulfill that purpose. Ifa offers solutions to that as well. As stated previously, the ultimate goal of Ifa is spiritual evolution through the maintenance of our ase. Your ase is maintained by allowing yourself to be a conduit of Divine Energy. As a conduit of Divine Energy you allow your creativity to flow and you are attentive to your inner voice, your needs, your wants and your desires. You become the person you were born to be, not the person society dictates to you that you should be. Remember as eniyan the fulfillment of your destiny is an integral part of bringing about the "good condition". Do not allow fear to keep you from being yourself, your Highest Self, your true self. If you do not become who you are supposed to be as Ifa sage and Babalawo (father of the mysteries)Sangogbemi Ajamu is fond of saying "you have robbed the world of your contribution" to the "good condition".

In order to remain a conduit, you must clear all blockages that obstruct the flow of Divine Energy within you. Blockages generally originate inside each individual. Clearing away these blockages requires spiritual, emotional, and physical transformation.

Let us look to nature for an example of what is meant by blockages. If we visit any flowing body of water; a river, creek, spring or stream; we will see areas where the water flows freely and areas where garbage and debris block the flow of water. As parts of nature we are no different. When we allow our minds, our bodies, our spirits and our lives to become blocked by trash and debris, we block the flow of ase. What constitutes trash and debris in life? The same things that constitute trash and debris in the creek. First there is garbage, useless waste that should never have been placed in the water in the first place. We put garbage into our bodies when we eat things that have no nutritional value, these types of foods block us in the same way plastic bags and soda cans block the creek. Foods high in nutritional value are also high in spiritual value and strengthen our connection to the Wombniverse. In addition to food, we also consume the music we listen to, the things we watch on television, and the conversations we participate in. If anything that we consume(be it food, music or conversation) is not uplifting, is toxic and/or of no spiritual value it will cause blockages. Participating in long conversations about other people and their issues and challenges is a tremendous toxic blockage. Pay close attention and you will see that anyone who spends most of her time discussing the business of others is not handling her own business! While removing these types of blockages keep in mind that things that bring you joy are spiritually uplifting. Pleasure is just as sacred and wholy as all other sensations. Remove the garbage and trash blockage from your life the same way you would remove it from the spring. Clear away all existing trash (internally that would mean the use of enemas, colonics, and/or cleansing herbs use Queen Afua's book Sacred Woman as a guide for this process) and stop putting trash into your life, your system, your body and your mind!

Second, there is natural waste that has accumulated in certain areas in the creek and is rotting; piles of leaves, sticks, and mud. The natural waste of life is the same stuff, things that were good for us initially but that have become toxic because they are stagnant, they are not growing, not moving, not

168

flowing with us towards our destiny. Natural waste in us takes the form of relationships that have outgrown their usefulness, jobs that no longer stimulate us, places, and spaces that we frequent out of habit that no longer feed our spirits or speak to our souls. Just like the spring sometimes these types of blockages can be shaken loose and will begin to flow with us, if after a time of trying to include them in your flow you see that it is useless (trust your inner voice on this, your Ori) clear them out of your path. In order to clear away these types of blockages we must exercise courage and not be afraid to trust our Ori to guide us properly. We cannot make the mistake of thinking that everything that is familiar to us is good for us.

Third, are the blockages caused by the way the spring carved its route out of the Earth. These blockages are caused by the land jutting out into the water and causing the spring to have to twist and turn. In life there are some obstacles that are a natural part of the course of life; they teach us strength and perseverance. Just like the spring, if we are diligent in moving along our path them we will eventually wear them away or learn to work harmoniously with them.

The more we study Ifa the more we will become aware of the glaring contradictions in our lives, those huge gaps that exist between what we claim to believe and how we actually conduct ourselves. Once these contradictions are made clear to us, it is the responsibility of each individual to right those wrongs. Each person is to be involved daily in being reborn or "reconstructed". Our Ancestors taught in the Wholy Odu Otura'Rete "Once I was initiated, I initiated myself. If we are given birth, we should bring ourselves into being again." This reconstruction of ourselves, this re-birthing is the duty of each and every Ifa adherent. If you are practicing Ifa and you are not making major, life altering changes for the better then you are allowing fear to keep you from fulfillment of your destiny. You are not being guided by the voice of your Ori. When we undergo these transformations, this evolution, we align our lives with our Ori. Once we are aligned with Ori we are able to fulfill our Divine Destiny.

You align yourself with your Ori by first cultivating a relationship with your Highest Self using the method described in the "How to Practice Ifa" chapter. After restoring the lines of communication between yourself and your ori you keep the correspondence strong through seeking Iwa Pele and balance in all of your endeavors and by being obedient to your Ori; by trusting the guidance of your Highest Self. Do not dismiss your own thoughts, wants, desires, and needs as unnecessary, or unattainable, or unrealistic.

Otura'Rete speaks of cultivating Iwa Pele in this way ...

"The balanced person. The moderate person.
One who knows moderation will not fall into disgrace.
I ask 'who knows moderation?'
One who is always working.
One who does not squander money.
One who dares not steal.
One who does not owe excessive debts.
One who does not drink liquor.
One who does not break commitments to a friend.
One who wakes early in the morning, meditates and thinks deeply about one's actions...

A balanced person is an ameso, one who is truly thoughtful in conduct."

The last two lines quoted (emphasis mine) explain the method our Ancestors used to achieve and maintain Divine Balance. They would awake early in the morning and meditate and think deeply about their actions. As discussed previously in the chapter entitled "How to Practice Ifa" it is by rising at dawn and saluting our Ori that we are able to "break the kola nut of ase". Breaking the kola nut of ase is tapping into our Divine Power, it is our magick. This simple act is what grants us the ability to make our dreams and aspirations manifest. This is what moves us into the realm of eniyan and ameso, the righteous individuals that we incarnated to become.

Odu teaches us that "human beings become Orisa". Those who

live righteous lives will be revered by their offspring. Those who continue to evolve and "reconstruct" themselves once they have become Egun will be elevated to the status of Egungun. As an Egungun if one continues to exhibit Iwa Pele one will be raised to the status of orisa. Life and the struggle to live it righteously does not end with death, the essence of life and the transformation of the essence continues forever, until we have become one with the All once more...only to begin the process again. This is why it is always Iwa Pele that we are seeking. Because it is Iwa Pele that will carry our spirits through the various transformations we need to make in the physical and spiritual realms. Remember the words of our Ancestors from the Wholy Odu Ogbe'Gunda "Iwa nikan l'o soro o" ;"Character is ALL that is requisite,o!"

How you act, what you do, how you conduct yourself in this life and in the life to follow is of PARAMOUNT importance in Ifa. Ifa is not a path in which the adherents are allowed to do wrong and then have the wrong-doings forgiven. The Universe does not work that way. If the river we spoke of earlier, runs through your town and is the major water source for your town and you pollute that river you will not have clean healthful water to use. You cannot go and apologize to the river for having polluted it and then expect it to miraculously become clean and healthy again. If you want clean healthful water again you must first STOP POLLUTING the river and then allow time for the river to go through the natural process that will allow it to cleanse itself. After that time, be it hundreds of years or thousands, the river will once again be clean and healthful.

Life is just like the river in the example. It is the responsibility of each individual to keep his own life as clean and pure as he possibly can. When one pollutes his own life, he should rest assured that he will feel the effects of that pollution until they have run their course. No amount of praying or begging for forgiveness can change that. Once a Universal Law is set in motion it will continue to move forward until it has reached it's Universally appointed stopping point. This is why the Ancestors said that "character is all that is requisite" and that it is Iwa Pele that we should be seeking.

The Ancestors warn that living without Iwa Pele does not mean that you will not acquire some of life's blessing but, according the Wholy Odu Ogbe'Tura...

"If we have money and do not have character,
The money belongs to someone else.
Character is what we are looking for character.
If we have children and do not have character,
The children belong to someone else.
If we have a house and do not have character,
That house belongs to someone else.
If we have clothes and do not have character,
Those clothes belong to someone else.
All good things that we have, if we do not have character,
These good things belong to someone else.
And so it is character that we are looking for, character."

It is lack of gentle character that causes one to lose all of the good things in life. Because it is lack of gentle character that steers one off of the path of her destiny. Lack of gentle character is a sign that one has forgotten that she is Divine in essence. One who exhibits this type of character continuously will not be revered by her offspring and thereby will not become egun or subsequently orisa. Those with poor character are out of alignment with the Universe and bring problems, illnesses, and poverty to themselves.

The goal of this life is to leave Aiye, the world, a better place than it was when you arrived. Each person will do this in his own way. Some are selected to raise healthy families, some are selected to heal the psychological and emotional wounds in the families they were born into, some are selected to create objects of art that remind others of their Divine essence. If you are living your life's purpose with Iwa Pele, then you are working towards achieving the "good condition". Everyone is not meant to be a prophet or a sage, but everyone was meant to exhibit the glory of the Most High in whatever their selected occupation may be. Remember it is through meditating, thinking deeply, removing your blockages and being guided by your Ori that you will come to know your Divine purpose.

To'
It is Enough
Conclusion

I was introduced to the Spiritual System of Ifa while finishing my undergraduate studies at Fisk University. I was taking a class called "The Black Experience in Religion". The instructor was Professor Ronald Summerville. During the class, he introduced us to ancient West Afrikan religious concepts and when he saw that my interest was peaked he brought a book to class and pointed out to me a short description of Oyotunji Village, a settlement of Ifa practitioners based in South Carolina.(Anyone interested in seeing Ifa in action should visit Oyotunji.) After reading that tiny paragraph, my Ancestors guided me to the campus bookstore where I purchased my first volume on Afrikan spirituality; Tell My Horse by the illustrious Ancestress Zora Neale Hurston (Iba ara torun). I have been a zealous student every since.

Ifa answered all of my questions and gave me a peace I had never known but had been praying for all my life. My spirit was renewed and my soul "opened up" I was indeed reborn. I grew up in the rural Southern portion of the United States in conditions not far removed from the sharecropping days of old. I did not stumble upon Black pride until matriculating at Fisk made it clear to me that we are a mighty, intelligent people; a force to be reckoned with. Even as I "converted" to Black militancy, I never dreamed that my Ancestors were the preceptors of practices so deep, so powerful, so mystical. Ifa brought to me an understanding of what it means to be Black and to be a woman on a Cosmic level. Ifa made me prouder than ever to be exactly who and what I am.

My prayer for this work is that it awaken men, women and children who are seeking to know themselves fully; just as Ifa as a Spiritual System has awakened me...

May you walk the path that has been created for you by your Ori,
May your righteous Ancestors continue to smile upon you and through you.
May you live your destiny fully and give birth to yourself in full.
May you enjoy your portion of ire(blessings) in this lifetime.
May you know love and experience peace.

May your mind, body, and spirit assist in bringing about the "good condition".
May you be the you that you incarnated to be.

ASE ASE ASE OHHHH!
TO'!

Recommended Reading

"Great wisdom is the key to gaining
great wisdom
If we do not have great wisdom we
cannot do great things"
Wholy Odu

Black Gods: Orisa Studies in
the New World
Adura   Orisa:Prayers   for
Selected Heads

Orin Orisa: Songs for Selected Heads

The first three titles are by John Mason; an absolutely INCREDIBLE scholar of Ifa and a gift from our Ancestors to all those who wish to learn more...

In the interest of space this list is short, and John Mason has blessed us by writing many more books on the orisa. Suffice it to say that anything written by this brother is HIGHLY recommended.

The Handbook of Yoruba Religious Principals
Baba Ifa Karade

Fundamentals of Yoruba Religious Concepts
Chief F.A.M.A.

Sixteen Mythological Stories of Ifa

Chief F.A.M.A.

Orisa Says Speak
How to Worship Your Orisa
Herbs of the Orisa
The above three titles are by Olaoluwa Fasade'. I HIGHLY RECOMMEND them. This author speaks in the sagacious, poetic voice of our Ancestors

Tell My Horse
Zora Neale Hurston

Divine Horsemen
Maya Deren

Macumba
Serge Bramley

Afrikan Woman: The Original Guardian Angel

Ishakamusa Barashango

A MUST READ for all Sistren!!! This book uncovers the true nature of the Afrikan woman, spiritually, politically, and historically.

Sacred Woman: A Guide to Healing the Feminine Mind, Body, and Spirit

Queen Afua

Without this book, my book would not be a reality! This is another MUST READ and also a MUST OWN for all Sistren. You DO NOT want to borrow someone's copy and then have to return it, TRUST ME! This book is a guide to a higher way of life!

When God Was A Woman
Merlin Stone

This is work is a historical study documenting the worship of the Most High as a feminine entity and how this worship precedes the belief in a masculine God.

Recommended Viewing

Quilombo: The first democratic nation in the Western hemisphere was the Black Nation of Palmares in Brazil. Created under the leadership of enslaved Dahomean queen Ago Time', Palmares was led by several members of the priesthood including the revered Zumbi whose birthday is national Brazilian holiday.

This film is the story of the Palmares.

Daughters of the Dust: The Gullah and Geechee peoples of the Sea Islands preserved West Afrikan heritage beautifully in every aspect of their lives. This film is the story of a Gullah family.

Sankofa: This film tells the story of the spiritual journey undertaken by a Eurocentric fashion model while she is visiting the slave castles in Ghana.

Recommended Listening

Olorun
Lazaro Ros

Lazaro Ros is a well know Akwpon(singer of orisa music). This is just one title he has to his credit.

Anything he sings is highly recommended.

Santisimo
Santisimo

A moving compilation of praise songs for the orisa.

Festival of the Deities
Chief Adebolu Fatunmise, the Gwanbaniyi of Ile-Ife

Chants to the orisa done in traditional Nigerian fashion by a world-renowned choral poet, singer, drummer and babalawo who hails from the place where the day first dawned, Ile-Ife. Baba 'Bolu (as he is affectionately known) is also the babalawo who initiated the author of this work.

Works Cited

Metu Neter Volume I: The Oracle of Tehuti

Written by Ra Un Nefer Amen, a sage and the high priest or Shekem Ur Shekem of the Asar Auset Society, this work is indispensable for in depth study of Afrikan spirituality from a metaphysical perspective. Any book by this author is a MUST HAVE for all serious students of Afrikan spirituality.

Olodumare:God in Yoruba Belief

Written by E. Bolaji Idowu this work is an explanation of Ifa as practiced in Nigeria from ancient times until now.

Let the Circle Be Unbroken

This monumental work by Mariama Ani explains the psychological, metaphysical, and historical implications of Ancestral Reverence. This author also has to her credit the work Yurugu.

Fundamentals of Yoruba Religious Concepts

A highly informative work by Nigerian native Ifa scholar who was "converted" to Ifa by the Ijo

Orunmila in Ile Ife. Chief F.A.M.A. is also living testament to the fact that women can be initiated into Orunmila in Nigeria!

Odu Ifa: The Ethical Teachings

A translation of the wholy odu of Ifa by the scholar who created the New Afrikan holyday Kwanzaa. This work presents the odu in Yoruba translates them in to English and then gives the author's perspective on the teachings.

About The Creatrix

195

I was born and raised in the rural Southern hamlet of Columbia , Tennesse...the sixth child in a family of nine. I attended Fisk University and received my Bachelor of Arts in English with a minor in African American Literature. I am a woman unapologetically and like all revolutionary Afrikan women, live my life from a womb centered, Afrikan centered perspective. I rely heavily upon the womanly arts of prayer, incantation, visualization, and attraction to guide me , nurture me and support me. I am the proud mother of six- five dawtas and one son. I have been unschooling my children for 19 years and have graduated two from my home school who are now on academic scholarships at Fisk University and Florida A & M.

I am a priestess/votary/avatar of the munificent mother Oshun and have been serving Her in this capacity since 1994. I offer counseling through the Merindilogun oracle, as well as coaching on home schooling and Afrikan centered parenting. For services visit my website :

http://osetura.wordpress.com/

Made in the USA
Las Vegas, NV
05 January 2021